KEY SKILLS FOR FCE READING

TERRY PHILLIPS
•
ANNA PHILLIPS

PRENTICE HALL
PHOENIX ELT

New York   London   Toronto   Sydney   Tokyo   Singapore

Revised edition published 1997 by
Prentice Hall Phoenix ELT
Campus 400, Spring Way
Maylands Avenue, Hemel Hempstead
Hertfordshire, HP2 7EZ
A division of Prentice Hall International

First published 1993 by Macmillan Publishers Ltd
© 1997 International Book Distributors Ltd

All rights reserved. No reproduction, copy or transmission
of this publication may be made save with written
permission or in accordance with the provisions of the
Copyright, Designs and Patents Act 1988, or under the terms
of any licence permitting limited copying issued by the
Copyright Licensing Agency, 90 Tottenham Court Road,
London, W1P 9HE.

Typeset in Novarese
by Microset Graphics Ltd, Basingstoke, Hampshire

Printed in the UK by Progressive Printing (UK) Ltd, Essex

Library of Congress Cataloging-in-Publication Data
British Library Cataloguing in Publication Data

A catalogue record for this book is available from the
British Library.

ISBN 0-13-2577674
ISBN 0-13-2584506 (with Key Edition)

5 4 3 2 1
01 00 99 98 97

The authors and publishers wish to thank the following who have kindly given permission for the use of copyright material:

BWB & Partners Ltd. for First National Bank advertisement, 1991: It should be carefully noted that this offer is no longer valid; Consumers' Association for an extract from 'How to complain about goods and services', 1992; Faber and Faber Ltd. for an extract from *The Story of English* by Robert McCrum, William Cran and Robert NcNeil, 1987; William Heinemann Ltd. for an extract from *An Old Captivity* by Nevil Shute, 1965; The Controller of Her Majesty's Stationery Office for extracts from 'The facts about children and roads', DOT, 1990, and Custom and Excise Notice 3, 'Bringing your belongings to the United Kingdom', Nov. 1987 and DVLA; National Geographic Society for an extract from 'The Disease Detectives' by Peter Jaret, National Geographic, Vol. 179, No. 1, 1991; The National Magazine Company Ltd. for an extract from 'Good Earthkeeping', *Good Housekeeping*, June 1991; Times Newspapers Ltd. for 'Girls will be girls and boys will be boys' by David Tytler, *The Times*, 10.5.91, and 'Darkest hour for midnight's children' by Tony Allen-Mills and Jon Swain, *Sunday Times*, 26.5.91; University of Cambridge Local Examinations Syndicate for the answer sheet on p. 74.

Every effort has been made to trace all the copyright holders but if any have been inadvertently overlooked the publishers will be pleased to make the necessary arrangement at the first opportunity.

The author and publishers wish to acknowledge, with thanks, the following photographic sources:

Barnaby's Picture Library pp 12 below centre; 32; Camera Press pp 12 above and below; 21, 41; Hulton-Deutsch Collection pp 27, 29; Popperfoto p 23; Val Randall pp 16, 17, 36; Alan Thomas p 44.

Illustrations by Peter Kent

The publishers have made every effort to trace the copyright holders, but if they have inadvertently overlooked any, they will be pleased to make the necessary arrangement at the first opportunity.

Key Skills for FCE Reading

Introduction

Overall Aims

This book has a number of overall aims:

1. to prepare students for the tests of reading in the FCE examination *as reading is tested* in that exam;
2. to provide a clear learning progression, with a variety of interactional patterns to enable both experienced and inexperienced teachers to produce highly effective, enjoyable lessons;
3. to provide the self-study student with a clear learning path and a way of checking progress.

To assist with aim 1, only authentic texts of the type used in the examination have been selected, and only tasks which will ultimately assist with correctly answering FCE Reading Paper questions have been set. In addition, the grouping of the texts with accompanying questions provides the teacher with easy access to revision/practice exercises of the same type as in the examination. In addition, most units have several EXAM WORK boxes which give specific advice on and practice in dealing with tasks in the examination.

To assist with aim 2, a highly structured 'lesson plan' approach has been employed.

To assist with aim 3, there are **Study Tips** throughout Section 1, a large number of closed questions, and a full, clearly referenced Key at the back for those using a **With Answers** edition.

Map of the Book

The book contains 12 units. Each provides three hours' classwork with additional homework tasks. At first, the reading passages will be relatively easy for students genuinely at FCE level, while students come to terms with the techniques.

The full texts are grouped at the back of the book.

Map of Each Unit

Each unit is divided into two sections. Any activities not completed in Section 1 can be set for homework and checked at the beginning of a subsequent lesson. Section 2 can either be done completely at home or in a subsequent class hour.

Lesson Goals

Each unit ends with a statement about the reading skills it is expected that a student has mastered.

Section 1: Improving Your Reading

Background Building Activities to encourage students to access useful 'frames' or 'scenarios' for the type of text to follow.

Activities to activate students' passive vocabulary in the content area of the text to follow.

Reading and Reacting Presentation of text in sections with a clear learning path through:

1. A variety of *pre-reading* and *while-reading* tasks encouraging:
   - hypotheses about content and function
   - prediction of how the information will be ordered
   - prediction of where hypotheses can be confirmed
   - checking whether hypotheses were confirmed
   - putting more detail on the prediction of content.

2. A variety of *post-reading* tasks focusing on the communicative value of each section of the text.

Section 2: Improving Your Vocabulary

Vocabulary is not explicitly tested in the FCE Reading Paper. However, vocabulary acquisition is a crucial component in the development of reading skills. This section contains a variety of practice activities enabling students to acquire knowledge of grammatical dependence and lexical relations:

- thematic sets
- discrimination of meaning between related items
- synonymy
- antonymy
- hyponymy
- polysemy
- collocation
- prepositional/phrasal verbs
- grammatical dependence.

Section 3: The Reading Texts

The Reading Texts
Exam-type Questions

Section 4: The Key

The Key with notes for all Sections 1–3 above for those using a **With Answers** edition.

Description of FCE Paper 1: Reading

Time: 1 hour 15 minutes.

The paper contains four parts. There are 35 questions in total on four long texts (or three long and two or more shorter texts). Parts 1 and 4 involve matching information, Part 2 is a series of multiple choice questions and Part 3 requires filling in a gapped text. The skills required include understanding gist and main points, picking out specific information, re-ordering jumbled texts and deducing meaning.

Contents

Introduction			5
Section 1	Improving your Reading		
	Unit 1	Mind that Child! *Text Type – Information Leaflet*	8
	Unit 2	The Train Journey *Text Type – Novel*	12
	Unit 3	Green Lights *Text Type – Magazine Article*	15
	Unit 4	Girls will be Girls *Text Type – Newspaper Article*	19
	Unit 5	Home Improvement Loans *Text Type – Advertisement*	23
	Unit 6	The Kennedy Conspiracy *Text Type – Documentary*	27
	Unit 7	The Disease Detectives *Text Type – Magazine Article*	33
	Unit 8	Fire! *Text Type – Information Leaflet*	40
	Unit 9	Death in the Family *Text Type – Novel*	44
	Unit 10	How to Complain *Text Type – Information Leaflet*	49
	Unit 11	An English-Speaking World *Text Type – Documentary*	54
	Unit 12	Coming to the UK *Text Type – Official Information*	60
	Practice Test		67
	Sample Answer Sheet		74
Section 2	Improving your Vocabulary		75
Section 3	The Reading Texts		88
Section 4	The Key with Notes; Sections 1–3 above (*with key edition only*)		105

SECTION 1 Improving Your Reading

 # Mind that Child!

BACKGROUND BUILDING

1 The text you are going to read was prepared by the British Department of Transport. How many words can you think of connected with transport? Write down as many words as you can in two minutes. Write them in two columns – **nouns** and **verbs**.

2 What do you think the *Department of Transport* is responsible for?

READING AND REACTING

A This is the headline of the text:

> **The facts about CHILDREN and ROADS**

B What could it be about?

C Here are some numbers that appear in the text. Can you guess what each one refers to?

1 1988   2 462   3 45,000

Read the first section of the text below and check your answers to **C 1–3** above.

✱ Road accidents are a major cause of death and injury to children. They account for a quarter of deaths of school children and for two thirds of all accidental deaths. In 1988, 462 children were killed in road accidents, and over 45,000 were injured.

✱ 1 in 15 children are injured in a road accident before their sixteenth birthday.

D What do YOU think?

1 How do you feel about this information?
2 How do you think the statistics compare with your country?

E Now complete these sentences with the correct numbers. The first is done for you.

1 The number of children killed in road accidents in 1988 was ___462___
2 The number of children injured in the same year was over _____
3 Road accidents account for _____ of all deaths of school children.
4 Road accidents account for _____ of all accidental deaths of school children.
5 The proportion fo children injured in a road accident before the age of 16 is _____

Exam Work

Text Type

In the examination you may be asked to say where a text has come from or what type of text it is. It is important to think about the text type while you are reading as this knowledge will help you understand the information in the text. In this case, where do you think the text has come from?

A a government leaflet
B an advertisement
C a book about road safety
D an official report

---

8 Improving Your Reading

Study Tip

Look for numbers in a text. The information they carry will often be checked in the comprehension questions. Underline them or highlight them and make sure you understand exactly what they refer to. The most common numbers are quantities, dates, proportions and ages. You should be able to make a sentence beginning with the number, e.g.

1988 is the year when...

462 is the number of children...

F Compare your answers in pairs.

G The next part of the text gives more facts about children and roads. Some of the sentences below come from the next part. Which ones? Explain why you chose each sentence.

1 Children in traffic are at greater risk of an accident than adults.
2 Children start school in Britain at the age of 5.
3 Children's observation and listening powers are less fully developed.
4 Girls tend to do better at school until the age of 13.
5 Most child pedestrians who are killed are knocked down by cars on residential roads.

H Now read the next part of the text and check your ideas.

∗ Children in traffic are at far greater risk of an accident than adults.

∗ Children's observation and listening powers are less fully developed and their stature means they are less likely to see and be seen.

∗ The overall risk of an accident increases as a child gets older. As pedestrians the risk is greatest when children start secondary school.

∗ Most child pedestrians or cyclists who are killed or seriously injured are knocked down by cars on residential roads carrying only light traffic.

I Some of the words in this section may be new to you. Can you guess what they mean *in this context*?

Example: 1 risk _danger_

2 observation   3 powers   4 stature
5 overall   6 pedestrian   7 residential

Check your answers at home with a dictionary.

Improving Your Reading 9

Study Tip

Do not read any text straight through. Pause after each paragraph and think: what is going to come next? This will make you check that you have understood what you have *already read* and it will also prepare you for what you are *about to read*.

Exam Work

In the examination you may be asked to match headings to paragraphs or sections of text. Look at the headings first and think about the kind of information that will follow. Then look for a section containing that kind of information.

J From your reading of this section, can you complete these sentences with something suitable? Again, the first is done for you.

1. Children in traffic are at far greater risk than ___adults___
2. Older children are more likely to have an accident than _____
3. The stature of children means they are less likely _____
4. More child pedestrians are killed on residential roads than on _____

K The final section is headed:

What can you do as a driver to make roads safer for children?

1. What *kind* of information do you expect to find in this section? Circle one of the words below:

   ideas   numbers   opinions   advice   orders

2. What advice would you give to drivers to make roads safer for children?

L Read the final section. See if the advice is the same.

* Recognise all children can be:

    Immature
    Impulsive
    Unpredictable
    Lacking in skill and judgement
    Inexperienced
    Irresponsible
    Unable to judge speed and distances

* Drive slowly in residential areas, particularly where parked cars may obscure your view.

* Slow down when you see children, even if they are acting sensibly.

* Slow down when you see a children or school sign.

* Watch out for children wanting to cross at zebra or pelican crossings and when turning at junctions.

* Give child cyclists plenty of room.

M Which word in this section from the right-hand column means the same as a word in the left-hand column? Draw a line between the two words. One is done for you.

1 remember   room
2 especially   sensibly
3 block   particularly
4 not stupidly   recognise
5 places where roads meet   obscure
6 space to move   junctions

7 You may know what a *zebra* is, and even a *pelican*, but what are 'zebra and pelican crossings'? Guess by starting with the noun – *crossing* – and then look back at the context in which zebra and pelican crossings are used.

N In the section which gives advice to motorists there is a list of **negative qualities** of children.
Don't look back at the section; can you remember which negatives began with:

1 Ir _____   2 Im _____   3 In _____   4 Un _____

5 How did the writer say that children don't have skill and judgement?
   Complete the sentence: Children can be _____ in skill and judgement.

   Check your answers with the text.

O Why does the writer give each piece of advice? Why should you . . .

1 drive slowly in residential areas?
2 slow down when you see children?
3 watch out for children wanting to cross the road?
4 give child cyclists plenty of room?

P Read the whole text again on page 88 and answer the questions that go with it.
For those with a **With Answers** edition, the Key to this unit begins on page 106.

In this Unit

...you have learned how to improve your skills in reading in the following areas:

understanding the purpose of the text; interacting with the text; predicting and comparing your ideas with the text - scanning for specific information; guessing the meaning of new vocabulary.

UNIT 2 The Train Journey

BACKGROUND BUILDING

1 The text you are going to read is from a novel written in 1940. The first few paragraphs describe a train journey in Western Europe.
What words connected with trains and journeys might be in the text?
Divide your list into **people** and **things**.

2 Look at the map of Western Europe.
Can you find these places? Are they near to each other?

Paris   Madrid   Geneva   Rome

READING AND REACTING

A Read the first line of the novel.

This case came before me quite by chance in the spring of last year.

B What is the profession of the writer? How do you know?

C Read the next sentence and check your idea.

I was travelling out to Rome for a consultation.

What do you think now? Why?

Study Tip

In first person narratives – *I went, I saw . . .* – it is important to think about who the writer is – name, age, sex, occupation. You often have to use the clues in the text to work out this information.

D Read the whole of the first paragraph and then answer these questions:

1 Where did the train start from?
2 Why didn't the writer go by air?

This case came before me quite by chance in the spring of last year. I was travelling out to Rome for a consultation. I might have saved time and fatigue if I had gone by air, but it was early in the year and I had decided against it on account of the high winds and rain. Instead, I booked a sleeper in the first class wagon-lit, and left Paris on the mid-day train.

E Can you guess the meaning of these words from the paragraph?

1 fatigue   2 sleeper   3 wagon-lit

F These sentences are *false*. Find the parts in the text which show that.

1 The *case* (which the writer is going to describe) was in Rome.
2 The writer finds plane journeys more tiring than train journeys.
3 The train journey would only take a few hours.

G Read the next paragraph and think about these things:

1 In what way did the journey stop being normal?
2 How did the writer feel about the train journey?

> The journey was a normal one as far as Dijon, and a little way beyond. But as the darkness fell and the line began to climb up into the Jura mountains the train went slower and slower, with frequent stops for no apparent reason. It was that difficult hour in a railway train, between tea and dinner, when one is tired of reading, reluctant to turn on the lights and face a long, dull evening, and conscious of no appetite at all to face another meal. It was raining a little; in the dusk the countryside seemed grey and depressing. The fact that the train was obviously becoming very late did not relieve the situation.

H Look back at the map of Western Europe on page 12. Draw the route of the writer's train.

I

1 How many words and expressions can you find which show the writer's attitude to the train journey?
2 What do you think is going to happen next? Read the next paragraph and check your ideas.

> Presently we stopped again, and this time for a quarter of an hour. Then we began to move, but in the reverse direction. We ran backwards down the line at a slow speed, for perhaps a couple of miles, and drew into a little station in the woods that we had passed through some time previously. Here we stopped again, this time for good.

J

1 On the sketch below, can you mark what the writer's train did?

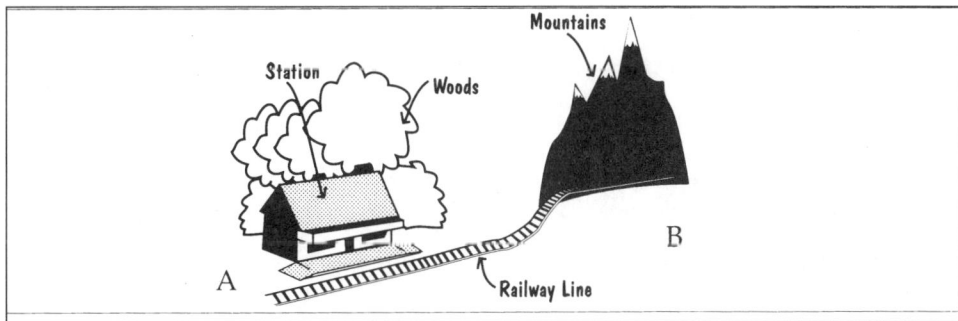

2 How long did the train stop at point B?
3 How far, roughly, is it from Station A to Mountains B?
4 'Here we stopped again, this time *for good*.' Does this mean the writer is pleased? What does it mean?

K If you were the writer, what would you do now?

Study Tip

In narrative texts like this one, make sure you know the order in which the important events happened. It helps to draw a map if people move from one place to another.

Read the next paragraph and check your ideas.

> I was annoyed, and went out into the corridor to see if I could find out what was happening. There was a man there, a very tall, lean man, perhaps thirty-five or thirty-six years old. He was leaning out of the window. From his appearance, I guessed he was an Englishman, so I touched him on the shoulder and said: 'Do you know what's holding us up?'
> Without turning he said: 'Half a minute.'

L
1. What nationality is the writer? Why do you think that?
2. Why did the writer *guess* that the man was English?
3. The man said '*Half a minute*'. Why?

M The train had stopped *for good*. Can you think of three reasons for this?

N Read the last paragraph and see if any of your reasons is the correct one.

> There was a good deal of shouting in French going on outside between the engine-driver, the guard, the head waiter of the restaurant car, and the various station officials. I speak French moderately, but I could make nothing of the broad, shouted vowels at the far end of the platform. My companion understood, however, for he drew back into the corridor and said:
> 'They're saying up there that there's a goods train off the lines between here and Frasne. We may have to stay here till the morning.'

O
1. How do you know from this paragraph that the man spoke French fluently?
2. Why did the man think they might have to stay all night?

P Read the whole text again on page 89 and do the multiple choice comprehension questions following it.
For those with a **With Answers** edition, the Key to this unit begins on page 107.

In this Unit

...you have learned how to improve your skills in reading in the following areas:

understanding the 'mood' of a text;
interacting with a narrative – predicting the story line;
guessing vocabulary from context.

UNIT 3 Green Lights

BACKGROUND BUILDING

1 The text you are going to read is from a magazine called *Good Housekeeping*.
This is a monthly magazine mostly for women which deals with topics such as family matters, cookery and consumer advice.
It is also very concerned with *green* matters.
What does *green* mean, in this context?

2 One 'green' issue at present is saving energy, in factories, on the roads, in the home.
Why do we need to save energy?
How can you save energy in the home?

3 These words and phrases are all connected with saving energy in the home.
Can you explain their connection with saving energy?

draughts   insulation   double glazing   thermostat

READING AND REACTING

A The article you are going to read is called 'Green Lights'. It is not about traffic lights.

1 What do you think it is about?
There is a picture with the article which shows three of the things mentioned.

2 Look at the picture and draw lines to connect each thing with the description below.

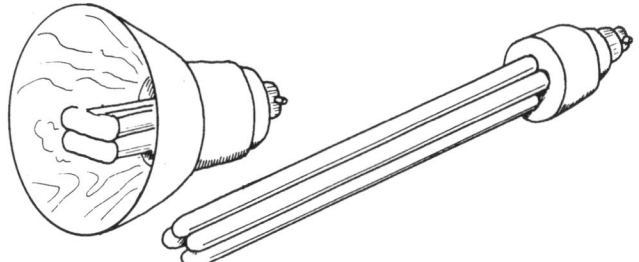

The Osram EL, pictured with reflector and globe

Exam Work

Purpose

In the examination you may be asked to decide why someone would read the text. It is important to think about the reader's purpose while you are reading as this knowledge will help you to understand the information in the text.

In this case, why would someone read the text?

A to find out how these lights work
B to find out where to buy these lights
C to check the prices of these lights
D to decide if they want to buy these lights

B The article contains factual information.
There is a common structure for articles like this.

First Paragraph(s)	Introduction of Topic General Facts	Section A
Middle Paragraphs	Example 1 Example 2 Example 3, etc.	Section B
Last Paragraph(s)	General Conclusion	Section C

Here are some sentences from the article. Which section do you think they come from, A, B or C? The first one is done for you.

Improving Your Reading 15

1   Energy-efficient light bulbs use up to 80% less electricity. __A__
2   Mazda Low Energy bulbs give white light for general lighting. _____
3   For a softer light, look for Philips SL Decor. _____
4   For a list of brands available by mail order, send a stamped sae to First Light, 28 Eastwood Road, Birmingham, B12 9NB. _____

C   Explain your answers to **B** above.

Example: 1 is 'A' because it's an introduction.

D   Now read the first paragraphs – *Introduction of Topic* and *General Facts*. Find the answers to these questions:

1   How much do energy-efficient light bulbs *cost*?
2   How much do they *save* (a) in money? (b) in electricity?
3   How long do they *last*?
4   How do they *work*?

Energy-efficient light bulbs use up to 80% less electricity and save you around £30 during their lifetime. They cost more than conventional ones – up to £15 – but last up to eight times longer. Carbon dioxide emission is also reduced.

• Compact fluorescent bulbs work the same way as fluorescent tubes but are bulb-shaped, so they can be used with ordinary shades, but not with dimmer switches.

E   What is it saying?
Decide whether these sentences describe advantages(+) or disadvantages(–):

1   Energy-efficient light bulbs use up to 80% less electricity...
2   ...and save you around £30 during their lifetime.
3   They cost more than conventional ones – up to £15
4   – but last up to eight times longer.
5   Carbon-dioxide emission is also reduced.
6   Compact fluorescent bulbs ... are bulb-shaped, so they can be used with ordinary shades, ...
7   ...but not with dimmer switches.

F   Vocabulary

1   What is the opposite of *energy-efficient* in this paragraph?
2   *Carbon dioxide* = CO_2. So what do you think the sentence means?
3   Can you guess the meaning of *shade* in this context?
4   *Dim* is the opposite of *bright* in this context. So what is a *dimmer switch*?

G   The middle paragraphs of the article now continue with some examples of energy-efficient bulbs. In the examples, there are names of various products from different companies.

1   How can you find 'product names' quickly in a text?
2   Look at the next three paragraphs and underline the product names. The first one has been done for you.

Study Tip

If you are reading a factual text like this one, draw lines to divide it into three sections:

Introduction/General Facts

Examples

Conclusion/Further information.

Study Tip

You must decide in a factual text whether the writer is saying something is:

a good thing or **a bad thing.**

In English, we normally group the good things in one section and the bad things in another.

Words like *and* and *also* tell you that the next item is of the **same sort**.

Words like *but* and *however* tell you that the next item is of the **opposite sort.**

You can usually decide whether the writer thinks something is good or bad, even if you don't fully understand the sentence. Knowing the writer thinks it is good or bad then helps you to guess the meaning.

> **Exam Work**
>
> In the examination you may have to choose the best place or product, etc., for someone. Look back at the paragraphs in **D** above and the three paragraphs in **G**. Which type of bulb would you recommend for someone who...
>
> 1 ...doesn't like fluorescent lights?
>
> 2 ...wants clear lighting over a large area?
>
> 3 ...wants a relaxing light for the sitting room?
>
> 4 ...doesn't like direct lighting?

- Mazda Low Energy (14W) bulbs give white light for general lighting. They contain a separate, reusable adaptor and a plug-in bulb. This works out cheaper as only the bulb needs replacing. (From supermarkets and lighting specialists, £9.99 for bulb and adaptor; £5 for replacement bulb.)

- For softer light, look for Philips SL Decor and for the SL Compact range (both about £12). With a rating of 18W or 25W, these bulbs enclose the fluorescent tube in a glass cover. Also look for the Osram EL (7W, 11W, 15W, 20W), £14-17 – available with a reflector or a globe cover.

- For uplighters and wall lighters, look for Philips Electronic range (9W or 11W), about £15, or the Osram EL. The fluorescent tube gives a good strong light behind your shade.

H There are two types of numbers in these paragraphs.

1 One set is obviously prices. What is the other?
W = Watts, and it is the way that electrical things are *rated*. It tells you how much electricity they use – the higher the number, the more electricity.
We talk about the *rating* of any electrical thing.

2 Do you know what the rating is of these conventional light bulbs?
(a) for a central light in the lounge
(b) for a table lamp in a bedroom.

I There is a table with this article which shows how much energy you save with the new tubes:

OLD FILAMENT	NEW TUBE
Nearest equivalent	
100W	20W
75W	15W
60W	11W
40W	9W

So what rating would you use with the new tubes?
(a) in the lounge
(b) in the bedroom

J Look back at the three paragraphs above and find the information to complete the table below. Some information has been entered to help you.

Product	Rating	Use	Cost
Mazda Low Energy			
		softer lighting	
	7W, 11W, 15W, 20W		
			£15

K These paragraphs give some extra information about the different products.

1 Circle the extra information in each paragraph.
2 All the extra information serves the same basic purpose. What is it?

L Remember! The final paragraphs bring the article to a conclusion.
In this article, there is only one concluding paragraph.
Which of the following pieces of information would you expect to find in this final paragraph?

1 more examples
2 advantages and disadvantages
3 how to get more information
4 other ways to save energy in the home

M Now read the final paragraph and check your idea.

● *For a list of brands available by mail order, send a stamped sae to First Light, 28 Eastwood Road, Birmingham, B12 9NB.*

N Vocabulary
Match words from the text with their meanings by drawing a line:

1 brands   *post*
2 available   *envelope addressed to yourself*
3 mail order   *products*
4 sae   *which you can get*

O Read the whole article again on pages 90–91 and answer the questions.
For those with a **With Answers** edition, the Key to this unit begins on page 107.

In this Unit

...you have learned how to improve your skills in reading in the following areas:

understanding the structure of factual text; scanning for specific information using illustrations and tables to assist in understanding.

UNIT 4 Girls will be Girls

BACKGROUND BUILDING

1 Do you think there are some occupations that only men should do and some that only women should do? Why?

2 Whatever we think, there are occupations that are mainly followed by men and others mainly followed by women.
Make a list of these in two columns:

        Men's Occupations   **Women's Occupations**

3 What about around the house?

(a) Make a list of *household chores*.
(b) Mark each one M if you think men usually do it
     and W if you think women usually do it.

Example: *washing clothes* ___W___

READING AND REACTING

A You are going to read a newspaper article about *stereotyping* – the way people put men and women into particular roles – in occupations and in the home.
The headline is:

Girls will be girls and boys will be boys...

The headline is designed to catch your attention. Here it refers to a common English expression, when male children do something naughty – *Boys will be boys*; in other words, you can't change the way they behave.

B Newspaper articles deal with two main types of information:

1 *news, current affairs*:   things which happened yesterday or last week
2 *general interest*:   things about life in the world today

This article is *general interest*.

Study Tip

Don't worry if you cannot understand headlines in English newspapers. They often contain jokes or they play with words. The article itself is usually much easier to understand.

Improving Your Reading 19

C General interest articles have a common structure. You met it before in the magazine article: 'Green Lights' (Unit 3).

First Paragraph(s)	a statement of the problem or situation – in an interesting way
Middle Paragraphs	more details and examples – in each paragraph
Last Paragraph(s)	conclusions/recommendations

D Because the newspaper wants to *catch your attention*, it does not give all the background details at the beginning of the report. Instead, this information is spread through the article.

This article is about a *report*. Look quickly through the article on page 92 and find the answers to these background questions. (You will also need to read the paragraphs which have been removed (A–F).)
1. When was the report published?
2. Who was it commissioned by? (three organisations)
3. How many children were questioned?
4. How old were the children?
5. How many teachers were questioned?
6. Which university wrote the report?

E Look back at the three organisations that commissioned the report.
Why do you think THOSE organisations are interested in stereotyping?

F As you know, there are two ways of quoting people or reports.

Direct speech   '_____.'
Indirect speech   he said (that); the report pointed out (that)

1. Look at the article on page 92. Find the direct quotations and mark the start // and end // of each quotation.
2. Who said the first quote?
3. Who said the other quote?

Note:
The people who said something are the *source*.

G In indirect speech, we can show that we are quoting by using quotation words like *said* and *told*. But we can also use other verbs.
How many quotation words or phrases can you think of?

H When we read an article like this, it is important to work out *who* said *what*.
Look at this example from the first paragraph:

> Boys and girls still see themselves as boys and girls, each with their own role to play. Most of them believe that boys repair cars while girls wash clothes, *according to a new report* published yesterday.

according to = the quotation phrase (Q)
a new report = the source (S)

20 Improving Your Reading

Look at the article on page 92. Underline the *source* and the *quotation phrases* and mark them with S and Q in the same way.

Notes:

1. The source + quotation phrase (or word) usually comes at the beginning or end of a paragraph. In newspaper articles like this one, the end of the paragraph is more common than the beginning. This is because the source is not as interesting as the information and means the newspaper can put the interesting information at the beginning.
2. In newspaper articles, a paragraph often contains only one sentence. The source therefore often applies to the whole paragraph which precedes or follows it.

> **Study Tip**
> Highlight direct and indirect speech in texts and connect it by a line to the source.

I The middle paragraphs give lots of examples to support the idea in the first paragraph – that boys and girls see themselves as having roles based on their sex. Sometimes words in the paragraphs help you to predict the kind of information that will come next.

Look at the words in a bold face in the first half of the sentences (on the left) below. Use them to predict which ending (on the right) should follow.

1. Children aged five and six have inherited the attitudes of their grandparents, **which...**   modern attitudes and the national curriculum

2. **Even where** children have seen jobs being done by both sexes, ... there is...   the latter mainly for men

3. The **former** (is) viewed as a preserve for women and...   a tendency to believe in stereotypes

4. Wearing trousers, shopping, and looking after somebody who is ill are the three roles most popularly considered to be right for both men and women, **but...**   are preventing more women from becoming scientists and engineers

5. The survey ... shows that divisions between the sexes exist **despite...**   children believe that only men should be scientists

J Sometimes *punctuation* helps to tell you what is coming next.
Sentences, and even whole paragraphs, often contain *lists*. Items in a list may be separated by a comma (,) or by a semicolon (;). You can tell when a list is about to end because the last item is introduced by *and*.

> Children have seen jobs being done by both sexes, such as teaching young children *and* doctors...

There are two items in this list:

> teaching young children
> doctors

1. How many lists can you find in the article on page 92?
2. How many items are there in each list?

Mark the text with 'L' – for list – and a number, for the number of items in the list.

K Sometimes there are no words and no punctuation to tell you what is coming next. But the structure of the paragraph or sentence gives you a good clue.

1 What sort of information do you think will follow this paragraph?

> Mending the car, fire-fighting, climbing mountains, woodwork and being a scientist are all seen as men-only activities by most girls and boys.

2 What about this sentence?

> Washing clothes was only for women, said 85 per cent of boys and 86 per cent of girls.

L Sometimes paragraphs are connected by the introductory phrase. Look at the way this paragraph begins:

> *Only one teacher* told the researchers: 'The boys tend to ....

The next three paragraphs are connected by their introductory phrases. How could they begin?

M

1 Now read the whole article on page 92 and complete the table from the summary below.

According to a new report from Manchester University, the majority of children aged five and six believe these occupations and jobs around the house are only right for men or only right for women:

	MEN	WOMEN
OCCUPATIONS		
AT HOME		

2 What solutions does the article mention?
3 What recommendations does the report make?

N Read the text on page 92 again if necessary and nswer the questions.
For those with a **With Answers** edition, the Key for this unit begins on page 108.

Study Tip

As you read any text in the exam, mark the punctuation more clearly. Colons tell you the next sentence is strongly related, commas often separate items in a list. Full stops, of course, start a new sentence. New paragraphs start a new idea.

Exam Work

You may be asked to replace missing paragraphs in a text. To help you decide where the missing paragraphs go, consider:

1 the overall structure of the text;
2 the previous paragraph.

In this Unit

...you have learned how to improve your skills in reading in the following areas:

understanding the structure of newspaper articles;
recognising the source of reported speech;
using punctuation to assist comprehension;
summarising the main points from a text.

22 **Improving Your Reading**

 # Home Improvement Loans

BACKGROUND BUILDING

1   The text you are going to read is about money. You need to know a number of words about money to understand the text.
Match the words below with their definitions by drawing a line connecting them. One is done for you.

insurance	money which you did not pay on time
loan	what the borrower offers to the lender
borrow	money you pay to protect yourself
lend	the extra money you pay to the lender
deposit	money you earn
instalment	extra pay for success, or special occasions
security	the first payment
interest	regular payment
bonus	payment for a professional service
overtime	give a loan
fee	money you pay – rent, electricity, etc.
arrears	money which you borrow
income	extra pay for longer hours
outgoings	take a loan

Now cover the words and try to remember them, from the definitions.

2   You also need to understand an abbreviation about money. The abbreviation is APR. Because there are a number of different ways of calculating interest, the government has said all loans must be quoted as an APR – the actual interest over one year. Therefore:

If APR is 10%, for every £100, you pay £10 interest per year.

3   The text is also about *houses*. What do we call…

a person who owns their house?
a person who rents their house?
a loan to buy or improve a house?
a person who lives in a particular area?

Exam Work

Text Type and Reader's Purpose

As you work through this text, think about

1 where this text has come from;
2 why someone would read this text.

READING AND REACTING

A

1   What's the difference between a *house* and a *home*?
The text you are going to read is an advertisement. The headline is:

TURN YOUR HOUSE INTO A MORE COMFORTABLE HOME

2   Look at the advert on page 93. What product is it advertising?
3   What is a *loan*?
4   How can you improve your home? Think of three ways.

B Before you decide to borrow money, there are many pieces of information you want to know.

Make a list of some of the questions you want to ask. If you cannot think of many, look at the questions in **F** on page 25.

Note:
Advertisements have two purposes:
1 to get your attention.
2 to give you information about a product or service.
An advertisement must get your attention **before** it can give you any information.
For this reason, it is sometimes difficult to read advertisements, to find out what they are about.

C In this kind of advertisement, you usually find these things. They are not always in this order!

> The *catch line* to catch your attention – often using the word *free*
> The *name* of the *advertiser*
> The *name* of the *product* or *service*
> The *headline* to make you want to read the advertisement plus sections which tell you:
> > *what* the product or service is
> > *why* you should buy the product or service
> > *how* you can get the product or service
> > *conditions* and *special offers*
> > *more information* or how you can get it
>
> There is often a *table* which summarises important numbers.
> There is often an *application form* to apply for the product or service or for more information.

Look back at the information you want to know in **B** above. Which section will you find each piece of information in?

D Here are the important words from **C** above.

> *why*   *how*   *what*   *headline*
> *conditions/offers*   *more information*   *catch line*
> *table*   *application form*
> *name of product*   *name of advertiser*

1 Write the words on cards.
2 Arrange them in the same way as in the advertisement on page 93.

E In this advertisement, there are a number of sentences with 'if'.
There are several problems about reading sentences with 'if'.
One problem is dividing the sentence into *condition* and *possibility*.
You must recognise where the sentence divides or you will not be able to understand it. Writers do not always use commas or even 'if'.

Study Tip

If you get an advertisement in the exam, check very carefully that you know *what product or service* it is advertising. Don't just look at the *catch line* or the *headline* – the things in *bold or italic type*. Find the *what* section. Sometimes the full name of the company at the bottom of the advertisement gives you a clue.

Example:

Condition: If you take out £7,500 over 180 months

Possibility: your monthly repayment at APR 21.5% variable will be £129.96

Find the 'if' sentences in the advertisement on page 93 and mark // where the condition ends and the possibility begins.

F Read the advert on page 93. Do *not* try to understand every word.
Find the answers to these questions.

1. Can I use the loan for whatever I like?
2. What security do I need to offer?
3. Can I insure the loan in case of illness?
4. What is the interest rate?
5. What is the maximum I can borrow?
6. What is the minimum I can borrow?
7. What is the maximum period for the loan?
8. What is the minimum period for the loan?
9. What happens if I die before the end of the repayment period?
10. How can I apply for this loan? (There are two ways.)

G Implicit Information

There is some information that is slightly hidden in the advertisement – because it does not help First National to sell its service.
Can you find the hidden information, or work out what it means?

1. What is the *danger* of a loan secured by a mortgage?
2. What is the implication of this:
   ...the APR is *variable* and is *currently* 19.7%.
3. What is the *limitation* on the offer of vouchers?
4. Why do you need to give information on income, outgoings and property?

H Below are some sentences from the advertisement. Can you guess the meanings of the italicised words? The definitions are all below. Put the letter of the definition after the sentence. The last one is done for you.

A	insurance	E	losing your job
B	house	F	reason for doing something
C	must pay	G	secret
D	price of service	H	easy to understand

1. Your loan will be secured by a mortgage on your *property*. __B__
2. For example, if you're under 60 you get Free Life *Assurance*... _____
3. ...on the total amount you *owe* up to £15,000. _____
4. There is even a special plan which enables you to insure your repayments – in case of illness, an accident or *redundancy*. _____
5. If you need any further *incentive*, we'll give you £150 worth of vouchers. _____
6. Call us...for an immediate *quote* and decision. _____

Improving Your Reading 25

7   You can fill in the *straightforward* application form. _____
8   The information is totally *confidential*. _____

I   Reading Tables

Look at the table underneath the headline.

All tables give information in *columns* – vertically – and *rows* – horizontally.

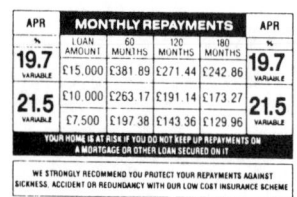

1   How many columns are there in this table?
2   Write the number of the column which contains this information:
    (a)   interest rate
    (b)   money you want to borrow
    (c)   monthly repayment for 10-year loan
3   How many rows are there in this table?

J   To read a table correctly, you always need to read vertically and horizontally – down a column and across a row.

For example, you want to borrow £10,000 over 10 years...

so find the column headed   Loan Amount
   find the row with   £10,000
   read across to column headed 120 months
   How much will you have to pay every month?   Answer: *£191.14*

Find the monthly repayments in these cases:

1   You want to borrow £15,000 over 5 years. _____
2   You want to borrow £7,500 over 15 years. _____
3   You want to borrow £10,000 over 5 years. _____

K   Sometimes you need to start with the figures in the boxes and work backwards.

For example, you can afford a maximum of £200.00 per month, so find monthly repayments which are under £200 and read vertically and horizontally.

What is the *maximum* you can borrow?   Answer *£10,000 over 10 or 15 years.*

Find the *maximum* you can borrow in these cases:

1   You can afford a maximum of £150 per month. _____
2   You can afford a maximum of £300 per month. _____
3   You can afford a maximum of £250 per month. _____

L   Read the whole advertisement on page 93 and answer the questions that go with it. For those with a **With Answers** edition, the Key to this unit begins on page 109.

Study Tip

Use tables which accompany texts to help you understand the text.
Label columns and rows more clearly if the abbreviated form is not helpful.

In this Unit

...you have learned how to improve your skills in reading in the following areas:

understanding the structure of an advertisement;
understanding implicit (hidden) information in a text;
scanning for specific information;
guessing the meaning of new words from context.

# UNIT 6 The Kennedy Conspiracy

BACKGROUND BUILDING

The text you are going to read is about something which happened in Dallas in the USA in 1963.

Quiz 1: Dallas

How much do you know about Dallas?

1. Is it a state, a city or a town?
2. Is it modern or old-fashioned?
3. Where is it?
4. How far is it from Washington?
5. Is there an airport there?
6. What happened there in 1963?
7. When exactly did it happen?

Quiz 2: American Politics

The famous event in Dallas in 1963 had an enormous effect on American politics. How much do you know about American politics?

1. What title is given to the head of the country?
2. What is the name of his house?
3. Which city is his house in?
4. What is one part of America called - e.g. Texas?
5. What title is given to the person in charge of each part?
6. Who was head of the American government in 1963?
7. Who did he beat in the election three years before?

READING AND REACTING

A Read the text on page 95 straight through. Try to find the answers to the questions in the two quizzes. Underline the phrases or sentences which contain the information.

B Whenever you read English, you will probably find there are words new to you.

1. What do YOU do when you meet a new word in a text?
   (a) ignore it
   (b) look it up in a dictionary
   (c) try to work out what it means

Actually, all three ideas are good, if you do them in the right order.

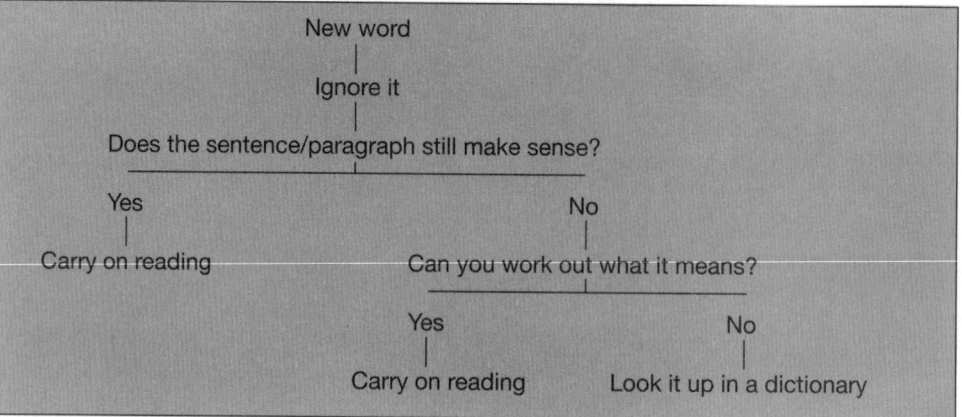

In the first three paragraphs of this article there are several words that are probably new to you. Let's try ignoring them. Does the sentence still make sense?

2. Put a tick in the space if the sentence still makes sense.
   Put a question mark if you need to understand the missing word.
   For example:

   In his office at the White House, the President looked ___✓___ across the desk at his press secretary, ... he said. The secretary replied, 'Don't worry about it. It's going to be a great ___?___ .'

Study Tip

In the exam of course you are not allowed to use a dictionary. You can only ignore a new word or try to guess what it means. So, from now on, do not use a dictionary at all in class, unless the teacher tells you to. Try to ignore or guess all new words.

Exam Work

Missing Sentences

You may be asked to replace a number of missing sentences in a text. One sentence will not belong in the text at all. You must learn therefore to identify sentences which do not belong. Throughout this unit, where you see a gap, decide which of the alternative sentences are missing.

Look at the sentences immediately before and after to help you decide.

For example, in **B2**, which of these is the correct missing sentence:

A I'm really looking forward to visiting Dallas.
B I wish I weren't going to Dallas.

28 Improving Your Reading

Exam Work

Missing Sentences

Which of these is the correct missing sentence? Why?

A The President didn't have to go.

B The President knew he had to go.

Now try to do the same for these two paragraphs.

It was November 20, 1963. The President had received _____ about Dallas from all sides. Senator William Fulbright had told him, 'Dallas is a very dangerous place. I wouldn't go there.' That morning Senator Hubert Humphrey had _____ him not to go. .... Dallas, a thousand miles away, had voted _____ for Richard Nixon in the last presidential election. This time round, the state of Texas as a whole was sure to be _____ for the Democrats, and Kennedy was determined to _____ .

Now look back at your question marks.

3 Can you guess...
(a) what kind of words are missing – verbs, nouns, adjectives, etc.
(b) if they are *positive* or *negative* ideas
(c) what the actual word might be

4 Here are the missing words. Put them in the spaces if you know where they go or look them up in your dictionary and then put them in the spaces.

trip   warnings   overwhelmingly
advised   tough territory gloomily
               take the initiative

Study Tip

If you can't think of the actual word in English, write in a word with the right meaning in your own language.

C Read the next three paragraphs from the article.
Complete Kennedy's itinerary from the information given in the text.
(Don't forget to deal with new vocabulary in the same way as **B** above!)

Date	Time	Action
November 21	morning	fly to _____
	lunchtime	speech about _____
	afternoon	fly to _____
	evening	speech about _____
November 22	early morning	_____
	then	_____
	late morning	fly to _____
	_____	arrive at airport
	then	drive to _____
	_____	arrive central Dallas

Improving Your Reading 29

Exam Work

Missing Sentences

Which sentence does not belong? What is the right place for the others?

A All went well there, and Kennedy made a speech about the space age.

B Just before noon, the President arrived in Dallas.

C The President had lunch and talked about the election.

On November 21 the President flew south from Washington to San Antonio, his first stop of the Texas tour. (1) .... He went on to Houston and talked about the space program again ...

November 22 began with a speech in the rain and a political breakfast. (2) .... There were welcoming crowds at the airport and then he was travelling to the city centre in an open limousine. As Kennedy passed, one spectator said to her husband, 'The President ought to be awarded the Purple Heart just for coming to Dallas.'

At 12.29 pm the motorcade was amidst cheering crowds, moving slowly through the metal and glass canyons of central Dallas.

D

Which word(s) in the section mean(s):

1 a large, luxurious car
2 a group of large cars
3 a large group of people
4 a person watching something
5 an American medal for bravery
6 shouting with happiness
7 deep valley (usually with steep or sheer sides)

E A *kaleidoscope* is a child's toy. It is a short tube with pieces of coloured glass and mirrors. When you turn the tube, the pieces of coloured glass move and the reflections in the mirrors change, making colourful patterns.

1 So what does the writer mean by *kaleidoscope* in this paragraph?

> For a while, there had been no talking in the President's car. Then, with the passing crowd a kaleidoscope of welcome, the wife of the Governor of Texas turned to smile at the President. 'Mr Kennedy, you can't say Dallas doesn't love you.'

2 Which of these sentences is closest in meaning to the Governor's wife's sentence?
   (a) Dallas doesn't love you
   (b) Dallas loves you
   Explain your answer.

3 Why did she say that?

F Read the last two paragraphs below.

Mark on the drawing:
1 the Texas School Book Depository
2 Dealey Plaza
3 Elm Street
4 the railway tunnel

> Ponderously, at eleven miles an hour, the procession moved on to Elm Street and into an open space. (1) ....
> .... To the right of the President towered the Texas School Book Depository, a warehouse, the last high building in this part of the city. In the lead car an officer looked ahead at a railway tunnel and said to a colleague, 'We've almost got it made.' (2) ....
> Then several shots rang out in rapid succession. According to a Secret Serviceman in the car, the President said, 'My God, I'm hit!'

Exam Work

Missing Sentences

Which sentence does not belong? What is the right place for the others? Why?

A Elm Street is a road in downtown Dallas.

B This was Dealey Plaza, a wide expanse of grass stretching away to the left of the cars.

C It was now twelve seconds past 12.30 pm.

G Several words in this section are used to emphasise size, speed, height.

1 Which word(s) emphasises...
   (a) the *width* of the grass in Dealey Plaza? (2 words)
   (b) the *height* of the Texas School Book Depository
   (c) the *speed* of the motorcade (2 words)
   (d) the *speed* of the shots (2 words)
2 What is another word for *officer* in this case?
3 What did the officer mean: 'We've almost got it made'?

H Finally, rewrite these sentences correctly to make a summary of the story. The first is done for you.

1. The President wanted to go to Dallas.
   The President didn't want to go to Dallas
2. Several Senators told him to go.
3. Dallas had voted for Kennedy in the last election.
4. Kennedy knew it would be easy for the Democrats to win next time.
5. Kennedy drove to Texas.
6. He went straight to Dallas.
7. The crowds were not pleased to see him.
8. He drove quickly through the city centre.
9. He was alone in the car.
10. Kennedy was shot after his car reached the railway tunnel.

I Read the whole article again on page 95 and answer the questions that go with it. For those with a **With Answers** edition, the Key to this unit begins on page 111.

In this Unit

...you have learned how to improve your skills in reading in the following areas:

understanding the structure of documentary narrative texts;
dealing with new words in a text;
transferring written information to a diagram.

The Disease Detectives

BACKGROUND BUILDING

1 The text you are going to read is from a popular American magazine called *National Geographic* about the discovery of the link between dirty water and cholera.
(a) What is *cholera*?
(b) And what is a *cholera epidemic*?
(c) Can you think of 20 other words connected with health and disease?
Organise your words into these groups:
   People   Places   Actions   Adjectives

2 Here is an illustration from the magazine article.
Can you name the object in the picture and the different parts?
What do you think the illustration represents?

READING AND REACTING

A The text contains certain pieces of information about a cholera epidemic.

1. What information would you expect to find in a popular science magazine article about a cholera epidemic?
2. Now look at the list at the bottom of this page (a–f) and check your ideas with this information which is in the article.

B In English writing, information about one particular point is put together into a **paragraph**. So each of the pieces of information above will be in a separate paragraph. Paragraphs contain one or more sentences about a particular point.
The *first sentence* of the paragraph usually tells you what the point is and, therefore, what the paragraph will contain. This first sentence is called the *topic sentence*.

```
Topic sentence_____
_____     } a paragraph
Other sentences about the same thing_____
_____
```

Look at some of the topic sentences from the text.
Match the topic sentence – 1 to 6 – with the information – (a) to (f) – which it introduces.

Example: 1 *No one knew how or why contagions spread.*

You probably don't know what *contagion* means (you may be able to guess).

Look at the rest of the topic sentence:

No one knew how or why...

Which of the areas of information is this paragraph going to be about?

Check the list – and you find in (c) the words – *ideas on the causes*.
Now try these. You should be able to do two or three more:

1. No one knew how or why contagions spread. __c__
2. 'We live in muck and filth,' they wrote to the London *Times* on July 3, 1849, _____
3. But a 41-year-old physician named John Snow believed he had found the source of the Broad Street contagion. _____
4. That was all he needed... _____
5. Although Snow did not discover cholera's cause – a bacterium called *Vibrio cholera* – _____
6. A man walking in good health, it was said, could be dead by sundown. _____

(a) living conditions in London in the 1850s
(b) description of the epidemic
(c) ideas on the causes of the epidemic
(d) search for and discovery of the cause of the epidemic
(e) end of the epidemic
(f) long-term result of the discovery of the cause

Study Tip

Highlight the first sentence in each paragraph. This sentence indicates what the paragraph is going to be about. If you understand this first sentence, it will help you to understand the whole paragraph.

Exam Work

Topic Sentences

Sometimes the first sentences in a paragraph will be removed. As we have seen, the first sentence is usually the topic sentence. It introduces the content of the paragraph.

C Once you know the *topic sentence*, you have a good idea of the *topic of the paragraph* which follows.
Once you know the *topic of the paragraph*, you have a good idea of the *contents of the paragraph*. In **B** above, 1 to 6 are topic sentences.
Decide which *paragraph* follows each *topic sentence* – (1) to (6) – above.
Mark them 1 to 6.

For example, the first topic sentence is 4: *That was all he needed.*

_____4_____ On September 7, Snow appeared before the vestry of St. James's Parish, meeting in solemn consultation on the causes of the epidemic. His request astonished them. He asked that the Broad Street pump handle be removed. It was. Within days the outbreak of cholera ended.

_____ Some blamed foul vapours. Others saw the work of divine retribution. Decades would pass before medical scientists accepted the idea that microbes too small to see were the cause of infection.

_____ Within 250 yards of the intersection of Cambridge and Broad Streets, more than 500 people died in little more than a week. Carts groaned under the weight of corpses carried away for mass burial. Those who could, fled. Others locked themselves away in fear.

_____ On a map of London, Snow marked where victims died. Nearly all the deaths, he saw, had taken place near the Broad Street pump – one of many public water pumps in London.

_____ in a letter signed by 54 of that city's poor. 'We haven't got any toilets, no dustbins, no drains, no water supplies, and there is no sewer in the whole place... We all suffer, and many of us are ill, and if the cholera comes Lord help us.' Five years later, in 1854, cholera came with a vengeance.

_____ his methodical work helped establish modern epidemiology, 'the art and science' as one of his present day counterparts would put it, 'of chasing epidemics.'

D Underline the words in each paragraph which helped you to decide which paragraph it was.

E Read the first part of the article again (see page 36). It is about:
   living conditions in London in the 1850s

1 Can you find:
   (a) two words for *dirt*
   (b) four words connected with *water*
   (c) a word connected with *rubbish*
2 Who are *we* and *they* in this paragraph?

3   ...*cholera came with a vengeance...*
    Do you think it was a serious epidemic or a mild one?

> 'We live in muck and filth,' they wrote to the London Times on July 3, 1849, in a letter signed by 54 of that city's poor. 'We haven't got any toilets, no dustbins, no drains, no water supplies, and there is no sewer in the whole place... We all suffer, and many of us are ill, and if the cholera comes Lord help us.' Five years later, in 1854, cholera came with a vengeance.

F Read the next paragraph. It is about:

description of the epidemic

1   Can you find...
    (a) two American English words...and give the British English words which mean the same?
    (b) an old-fashioned vehicle?
    (c) a word for *dead bodies*?
    (d) a word meaning *all together*?
    (e) a word meaning *ran away*?
2   *Carts groaned...*
    What did the carts actually do?
3   *Others locked themselves away in fear.*
    Fear of what?

> A man walking in good health, it was said, could be dead by sundown. Within 250 yards of the intersection of Cambridge and Broad Streets, more than 500 people died in little more than a week. Carts groaned under the weight of corpses carried away for mass burial. Those who could, fled. Others locked themselves away in fear.

G The next paragraph is about:

ideas on the causes of the epidemic

It is quite complicated. Here is a simpler summary of the ideas. Find the words in the paragraph which mean the same as the sections in italics.

Underline and number them in the paragraph. The first is done for you.

1   People didn't know *the cause of epidemics*.

> 1
> No one knew <u>how or why contagions spread</u>. Some blamed foul vapours. Others saw the work of divine retribution. Decades would pass before medical scientists accepted the idea that microbes too small to see were the cause of infection.

2   Some people thought it was *bad air*.
3   Others thought it was *the work of God*.
4   *It was many years* before people realised that...
5   ...*tiny germs* caused the disease.

H So, what do you think these words mean?
Match the words on the left with their meanings on the right by drawing a line to connect them. One has been done for you.

contagions	air
blame	periods of ten years
foul	germs
vapours	from God
divine	epidemics
decades	bad
microbes	say it is the fault of
infection	passing disease from one person to another

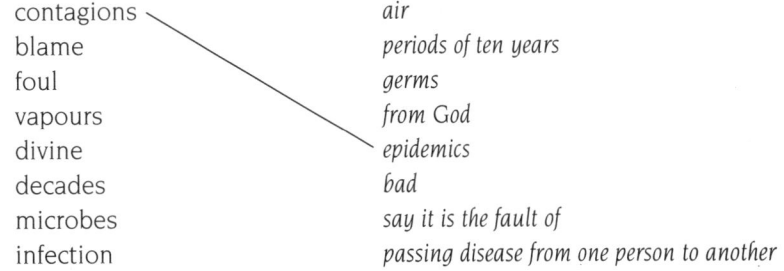

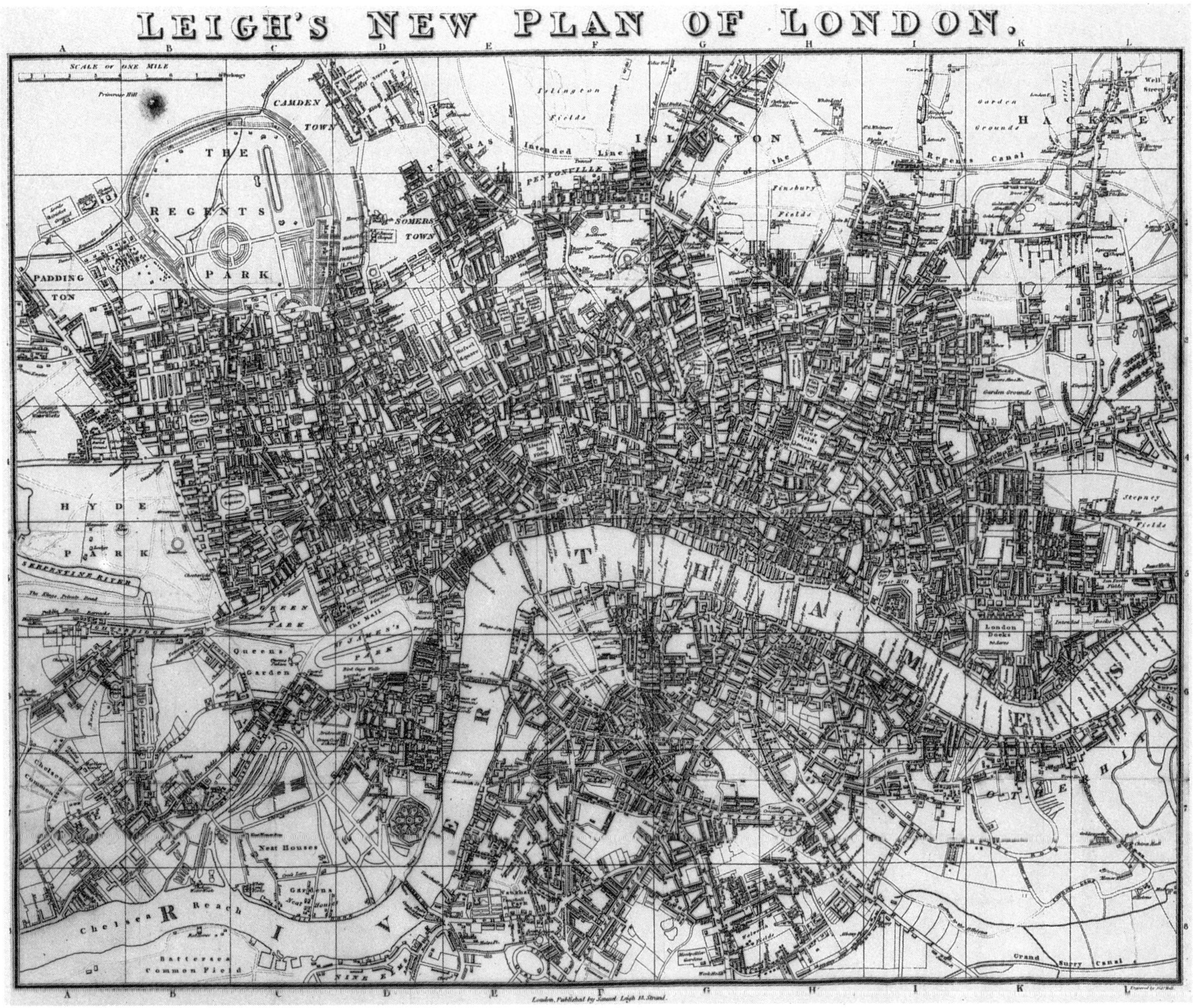

1 The rest of the text is about John Snow:

   his *search for the cause* of the epidemic
   and *his discovery* of the cause
   the *end* of the epidemic
   and the *long-term result* of the discovery of the cause.

Improving Your Reading 37

> **Study Tip**
>
> Third person narratives – stories told with *he, she, they* – are more difficult to understand than first person *I* because it is possible to refer to people in different ways.
>
> When you are reading a text like this, underline the nouns and pronouns that refer to the main character. If there are two, use two different colours.
>
> Remember! You can refer to a person with their name (first, surname, both), their occupation, age or physical characteristics. In English documentary narrative you will often find a pattern of reference like this: name-he-he-name-he-he-name, etc.

1. Read the text and underline all references to John Snow.

> But a 41-year-old physician named John Snow believed he had found the source of the Broad Street contagion. On a map of London, Snow marked where victims died. Nearly all the deaths, he saw, had taken place near the Broad Street pump – one of many public water pumps in London.
>
> But before he could be sure, Snow had to understand why ten deaths had occurred nearer another street pump. Amid the growing panic, Snow visited the families of the deceased. Five of the distant victims, he learned, regularly sent for water from the pump at Broad Street, preferring its taste. Three others were children who attended a school near Broad Street's pump.
>
> That was all he needed. On September 7, Snow appeared before the vestry of St. James's Parish, meeting in solemn consultation on the causes of the epidemic. His request astonished them. He asked that the Broad Street pump handle be removed. It was. Within days the outbreak of cholera ended.
>
> Although Snow did not discover cholera's cause – a bacterium called Vibrio cholera – his methodical work helped establish modern epidemiology, 'the art and science' as one of his present day counterparts would put it, 'of chasing epidemics'.

2. You should have found 16. Check with the person next to you if not.

J There are some words in this section which are probably new to you. But in many cases it is possible to guess from the context what they mean.

Example: *victim*

Out of context you either know the word or you don't.
But in the sentence from the article it is possible to guess at least part of its meaning...

> On a map of London, Snow marked where victims died.

Are *victims* things or people? _____
Are they alive or dead? _____
Why did they die? _____
What, then, is a victim? _____

In fact a *victim* is someone who is involved in any problem which causes pain or suffering. Sometimes a victim dies, sometimes not. But from the context you can get a good idea of the meaning.

1. Now try these. Look at the context and ask yourself questions, as in the example above:
   (a) pump
   (b) panic
   (c) deceased
   (d) distant
   (e) vestry
   (f) in solemn consultation
   (g) outbreak
   (h) bacterium
   (i) epidemiology
   (j) counterparts

> **Study Tip**
>
> The multiple choice questions often ask you *why* something happened, especially in sentences such as:
> *John Snow asked them to remove the handle of the pump because...*
> It is very rare that the correct reason is directly stated in the text.
> So, while you are reading, keep asking yourself – WHY?

2   Check your ideas with the person next to you. Then look the words up in a dictionary.
3   True (T) or False (F)?
    Answer these true or false sentences about John Snow. The first is done for you.
    (a) He marked a map with the places people had died. __T__
    (b) He visited the families and panicked. ____
    (c) He regularly sent for water from the Broad Street pump. ____
    (d) He spoke to the vestry of St. James's Parish. ____
    (e) He removed the Broad Street pump handle. ____
    (f) He discovered the cause of cholera. ____

K   Now read again the full text on pages 95–96.

Notice especially the words:

some, other(s),   nearly all,   five of the...

You will need them to answer some of the questions in the next section.
Now find the answers to these questions.

1   What problems did the poor people of London mention in their letter? (5 things)
2   What did people living near Cambridge Street and Broad Street do? (3 things)
3   What did people blame for the contagion? (2 things)
4   Where did the deaths occur? Complete the sentence:
    (a) Nearly all _____
    (b) but ten _____
5   What did John Snow discover about the 10 deaths which occurred near another street pump? Complete the sentences:
    (a) Five of the victims _____
    (b) Three others _____
    (c) and the other two? _____
6   What was the meeting on September 7th about?

L   Implicit Information
Without reading the text again, can you answer these WHY questions about the information in the text? Be careful! None of the answers is given directly in the text.

1   Why did the poor of London fear cholera in the 1850s?
2   Why did 500 people die near the intersection of Cambridge and Broad Streets?
3   Why didn't scientists in the 1850s know the true cause of contagion?
4   Why did John Snow mark on a map the places where victims had died?
5   Why did the 10 people who didn't live near the Broad Street pump die?
6   Why did John Snow ask for the Broad Street pump handle to be removed?
7   Why did the outbreak of cholera stop?
8   Why is John Snow's work important in medical history?

M   Read the text on pages 95–96 again and do the multiple choice comprehension questions which follow.
For those with a **With Answers** edition, the Key to this unit begins on page 112.

In this Unit

...you have learned how to improve your skills in reading in the following areas:

understanding paragraph structure;
understanding topic sentences;
predicting information from discourse markers;
recognising referents.

UNIT 8 Fire!

BACKGROUND BUILDING

1   The text you are going to read is about fire.
Make a list of the words you know connected with fire.

2   The text is an extract from a safety leaflet called:

> **HOW TO SURVIVE A HOTEL FIRE**

If you *survive* something, what happens to you...or perhaps, what doesn't happen to you?

3   List the reasons why a fire *in a hotel* might be more dangerous than a fire in *your own home*.

READING AND REACTING

A   What is the most likely cause of death in a hotel fire?

B   Read the first section and check your ideas.

> Contrary to what you may have seen on television or in the movies, fire is not likely to burn you to death. It's the by-products of fire that will kill you.

Think! What are the *by-products of fire*?

C   Read the next part and check your ideas.

> Super heated fire gases (smoke) and panic will almost always be the cause of death long before the fire arrives, if it ever does. This is very important. You must know how to avoid smoke and panic to survive a hotel fire. With this in mind, here are a few tips.

40 Improving Your Reading

Study Tip

We have seen that the first sentence of a paragraph helps you to anticipate what information the paragraph will contain.

In many cases, the *last sentence* of a paragraph helps you to predict what the *next paragraph* will contain – and in what order.

After you read the last sentence of a paragraph, pause for a moment and think what will come next.

Exam Work

Audience

In the examination you may be asked who a text has been written for. It is important to think about the audience for the piece of writing as it helps you to understand the contents.

In this case, who do you think the article has been written for?

A hotel staff
B hotel guests
C fire fighters
D first aid people

D
1   What, in simple English, is *super heated fire gases*?
2   And what is the other common cause of death in hotel fires?
3   How can these things kill you?

E   Look back at the last two sentences of the passage above.
1   What is the next part of the text going to be about?
2   Which information will come first: *panic* or *smoke*?
3   Why?
4   Can you give any *tips*:
    (a) to avoid *smoke*
    (b) to avoid *panic*

F   Read the next part and check your ideas.

Smoke
Where there is smoke there is not necessarily fire. A smouldering mattress, for instance, will produce great amounts of smoke. Air conditioning and air exchange systems will sometimes pick up smoke from one room and carry it to other rooms or floors. You should keep that in mind because 70 per cent of hotel fires are caused by smoking and matches.

In any case, your prime objective should be to leave the hotel at the first signs of smoke.

G   There is a saying in English:

Where there's smoke, there's fire.

1   Can you guess what it means?
    Do you have anything similar in your language?
2   What does the writer mean...

    Where there is smoke there is not necessarily fire.

3   You wake up. There is smoke in your room. Where could it have come from, according to this passage?
4   Why does the writer point out that the smoke could have come from another room?
5   So, is the writer saying smoke is not dangerous? Explain your answer.

H   The next section explains *problems* with smoke, and *solutions*.
Read the section and say whether the information is a problem or a solution.

Smoke, being warmer, will start accumulating at the ceiling and work its way down. The first thing you will notice is there are no 'exit' signs.

Another thing about smoke you should be aware of is how irritating it is on the eyes. The problem is your eyes will take only so much irritation, then they close. Try all you want, you won't be able to open them if there is still smoke in the area.

Lastly, the fresh air you want to breathe is at or near the floor. Get on your hands and knees (or stomach) and STAY THERE as you make your way out. Those who don't probably won't get that far.

Study Tip

It is not enough to understand all the words in a sentence. You must understand what the sentence is doing in that place. Is it describing a problem, or a solution; an advantage or a disadvantage? Look for markers in a text which join sentences with the same purpose, e.g. *Another thing...; also...; in addition*.

1 Put P for Problem or S for Solution beside these ideas. The first one is done for you.
   (a) Get on your hands and knees ___S___
   (b) Your eyes close _____
   (c) Fresh air is at or near the floor _____
   (d) Smoke irritates your eyes _____
   (e) There are no 'exit' signs _____

2 Why...
   (a) Why does smoke accumulate at the ceiling?
   (b) Why are there no exit signs?
   (c) Why is smoke irritation such a problem?
   (d) Why should you get on your hands and knees (or stomach)?

I The final section is headed:

If you are forced to stay in your room

Look at the illustration which goes with the next part of the text.

Can you give advice to go with each picture?

Example: 1 *You should put a handkerchief over your nose and mouth.*

J Now read the final section on the next page and mark the advice in the text 1 to 7. Number 1 is done for you.

42 Improving Your Reading

Should you wake up to smoke in your room and the door is too hot to open or the hallway is completely charged with smoke, don't panic. Many people have defended themselves quite nicely in their rooms and so can you. One of the first things you'll want to do is <u>open the window</u> (1) to vent the smoke. If there is fresh air outside, leave the window open, but keep an eye on it. At this point, most people would stay at the window, waving frantically, while their room continues to fill with smoke or the fire burns through. You must be aggressive and fight back.

Here are some things you can do in any order you choose: If the room phone works, let someone know you're in there. Flip on the bathroom vent. Fill the tub with water. Wet some sheets or towels and stuff the cracks of your door to keep out smoke. With your ice bucket, bail water from the bathtub on the door to keep it cool. Feel the walls; if they're hot, bail water on them too. You can put your mattress up against the door and block it in place with the chest. Keep it wet: keep everything wet. A wet towel tied around your nose and mouth is an effective halter if you fold it in a triangle and put the corner in your mouth. The point is, there shouldn't be any reason to panic; keep fighting until reinforcements arrive. It won't be long.

K Some words in this section are unusual, or used in a strange way. Can you guess their meanings in this context? Join words and meanings. One is done for you.

1	should	hold
2	charged	turn
3	nicely	cupboard with drawers
4	vent	mask
5	frantically	other people (probably firemen)
6	flip	carry and pour
7	stuff	well
8	bail	if
9	block	filled
10	chest	let out
11	halter	in a panic
12	reinforcements	fill up

(line drawn from 2 charged to filled)

Study Tip

English words often have several meanings. If a sentence doesn't make sense to you, even though there are no 'new' words in it, consider whether one of the familiar words is being used in a new way. e.g. *should* meaning *if* in this case.

L Why *should* you...
1 open the window? _____ to let the smoke out _____
2 use the phone? _____
3 fill the bathtub? _____
4 fill up the cracks of the door? _____
5 put water on the door? _____
6 put a wet towel over your nose and mouth? _____

M Why *shouldn't* you...
1 stay at the window? _____
2 panic? _____

N Now read the whole text again on page 97 and answer the questions that go with it. For those with a **With Answers** edition, the Key to this unit begins on page 114.

In this Unit

...you have learned how to improve your skills in reading in the following areas:

recognising the purpose of sentences
using discourse structure to assist with comprehension
understanding common words used in unusual ways

Improving Your Reading 43

UNIT 9 Death in the Family

BACKGROUND BUILDING

1 Some texts in the FCE examination are taken from popular novels. It is useful to be able to work out what kind of novel it is from. There are some things which will help you:

the occupations of the people in the novel	– the *characters*
where they are	– the *locations*
what they do	– the *events*
the particular words	– the *vocabulary* that is connected with that type of novel

If you know what type of novel you are reading, it is much easier to anticipate what is going to happen and to understand the text.

2 Below are the names of some types of novel.

    crime   western   romance   horror
    adventure   science fiction   historical

For each type of novel, can you think of:

two *occupations* for the characters
two *locations*
two *events*
two *vocabulary* items

The first one has been done as an example:

Type	Occupations	Locations	Events	Vocabulary
crime	policeman detective	bank dark street	murder robbery	gun investigation

READING AND REACTING

A The exercises here will help you to understand the *gist* of the text. We will not look at individual words or phrases here and you should not use your dictionary for words you do not understand. We shall look at vocabulary in Section 2, Improving Your Vocabulary.

The text you are going to read is from the first chapter of a novel. Read the first sentence of the novel:

    The body lay on a small square of carpet in the middle of the gun-room floor.

Think of three questions you want to know the answers to now, having read this first sentence.

B Read the next sentence.

1 Are any of your questions in **A** above answered?

    Alec Chipstead looked around for something to put over it.

Study Tip

If you recognise that the text is from a novel, read the text straight through without worrying about words or sections that you don't understand. The important thing during the first reading is to get a general idea of the story line. This is called the *gist*.

44 Improving Your Reading

2   Think of another question you want to find the answer to now.

C   Read the rest of the first paragraph.

1   Are you surprised at the man's actions? Why/why not?
2   Do his actions help to answer any of your questions in **A** and **B** above?

> He unhooked a raincoat from one of the pegs and, covering the body, reflected too late that he would never wear that again.

3   What would he never wear again? Why?

D   The structure of this passage is typical of novel style when a writer is describing actions which happened 1, 2, 3.

> He **did** something and, **doing** a second thing, **did** a third thing.

What were the three actions that Alec did?

E   There is one word in the next section that will probably answer most of your questions. But don't worry if you don't understand it. There is another word you certainly know which will also help.

Underline the two important words.

> Alec went outside to see the vet off.
> 'I'm glad that's all over.'
> 'Extraordinary how painful these things can be,' said the vet. 'You'll get another dog, I suppose?'
> 'I expect so. That's really up to Meg.'

F   Can you answer these questions now? (Some of them may be the same as your questions in **A** and **B** above.)

1   Whose body is it?
2   How did it die?
3   Who is Alec Chipstead?
4   Who is Meg?

Note:
In this text, you may not be sure of the following vocabulary so far:

| gun-room | unhook | peg | extraordinary |
| vet | reflect | up to | see off |

We shall look at them in Section 2.

G   In order to understand the things in the **Study Tip** left, it is sometimes helpful to:

> Draw a 'family tree' of people and relationships – WHO
> Draw a 'time line' of actions – WHAT and WHEN
> Divide this up into WHERE actions happened
> Try to say WHY each thing happened

How much information can you fill in for each section from the text so far?
Write these words in your notebooks and fill in as much as you can.

WHO   WHAT and **WHEN   WHERE   WHY**

Study Tip

In the examination there are often texts from novels or stories. When you are reading stories or parts of stories it is very important that you work out:

Who are the main characters?
What is their relationship to each other?
Where are they?
What are the main things they do during the text?
Why do they do these things?

It is a good idea to do this *before* you try to work out the exact meaning of new words, or familiar words used in a new way.

Study Tip

Keep checking that you have the right relationships, the right order for the actions and the right reason for those actions.

If you do these things while you are reading, you will probably find that you understand more, including the meanings of new words, because you are anticipating the next piece of information, trying to fit it into the diagrams.

H Stories and novels often contain detailed descriptions of people or places. Read the next paragraph.

1 Draw lines — // — to separate the two types of information in this paragraph.
   (a) actions
   (b) descriptions

   The vet nodded. He got into his car, put his head out of the window and asked Alec if he was sure he didn't want the body taken away. Alec said, no, thanks, really, he'd see to all that. He watched the car move off, up the long, sloping lane that in those parts was called a drift, under the overhanging branches of the trees, and disappear round the bend where the pine wood began.

2 Add the new action to the 'time line' below:

   WHAT and WHEN _____
                    the dog died   Alec covered it   the vet...

3 What is the description in the second part of the paragraph about?
   (a) the car
   (b) the lane
   (c) the trees
   (d) the bend
   (e) the wood
   It is usually not important that you understand every word in a description exactly. You do need to get a general picture of what the writer is describing.

4 Is Alec's house...
   (a) in the country?
   (b) in a town?

5 Is the lane...
   (a) long and dark?
   (b) short and steep?
   (c) wide and open?

Note:
There are some more words and phrases you may not be sure of:
   sloping   lane   overhanging   pine
We shall look at them in Section 2.

I In the next section, there is one very unusual type of sentence. There are also several words that will probably be new to you. However, it is still easy to get an idea of the important actions.

1 Alec did one thing in this section (or maybe two!). What did he do?

   On the edge of the grass, where a strip of flower border separated it from the paved drive, lay a rubber ball dented with toothmarks. How long had that been there? Months probably. It was a long time since Fred had been up to playing with a ball. Alec put it into his pocket.

Study Tip

Don't worry about understanding every word in a long description. Just get a general idea of what is being described.

46 Improving Your Reading

2   The rest of the paragraph is about the ball.
    (a) Where did Alec see it?
    (b) Whose ball was it?
    (c) Why was it dented?
    (d) Why hadn't Fred played with it for a long time?

J   Look at this sentence. It contains the same information as one part of the text:

   The ball lay on the grass.

What order does the writer give this information in the paragraph?

Note:
The normal order for information in a sentence in English is:

   Subject   **Verb**   **Prepositional Phrase**
   The ball   *lay*   *on the grass*

But if we begin a sentence with the preposition we can reverse the order of subject and verb:

   Prepositional Phrase   **Verb**   **Subject**
   On the grass   *lay*   *the ball*

When you find a sentence that begins with a preposition, be prepared for the verb to come before the subject.

K   The sentences below are not quite true.

1   Read the paragraph and correct them.
    (a) Alec climbed into the house through a window.
    (b) Meg was reading a magazine.
    (c) Fred, the dog, went to sleep.

> He walked round the house, up the stone steps onto the terrace and in by the French windows.
> Meg was sitting in the drawing room, pretending to read *Country Life*.
> 'He didn't know a thing,' Alec said. 'He just went to sleep.'
> 'What fools we are.'
> 'I held him on my lap and he went to sleep and the vet gave him the injection and he – died.'

2   Are you sure now...?
    (a) Who is Mcg?
    (b) What happened to Fred?
    (c) Why?

L   Who did what?

1   Read the story on page 98 straight through once more.
2   Now do this exercise.
    Below are the characters in this text and the important actions.
    Match the characters to the actions:
    Alec   Meg   Fred   the vet

    (a) _____ got into his car.
    (b) _____ asked if he wanted the body taken away.
    (c) _____ covered the body.
    (d) _____ put the ball in his pocket.

Improving Your Reading 47

(e) _____ was pretending to read a magazine.
(f) _____ went into the house.
(g) _____ and _____ went outside.
(h) _____ held him on his lap.
(i) _____ said he would see to the body.
(j) _____ lay on the carpet.
(k) _____ went to sleep.
(l) _____ gave him an injection.

3 Now put the actions in the correct order.

M We can check the vocabulary now in Section 2, page 83.

Answer the accompanying questions *without* rereading the text on page 98.
For those with a **With Answers** edition, the Key to this unit begins on page 115.

In this Unit

...you have learned how to improve your skills in reading in the following areas:

recognising different types of novel; skimming to get a general idea of the gist; recognising descriptions in the middle of narrative.

48 Improving Your Reading

How to Complain

BACKGROUND BUILDING

1   The text extracts you are going to read are about buying and selling things.
There are many words in English which mean:
   (a) someone who *makes* or *sells* something
   (b) someone who *buys* or *uses* something
Make two columns, headed (a) and (b). Put the words below into the correct column.

*buyer   seller   manufacturer   customer   consumer
purchaser   vendor   retailer   producer
trader   client   assistant   dealer*

2   The text is from a consumer magazine called W*hich*? This magazine gives people advice on what thing to buy to get the best value. It also gives advice on what to do if things go wrong.
This section is from 'How to Complain about Goods' and it begins with an example:

   A typical example: you buy a pair of shoes in a sale. A week later a strap comes right away making the shoes unwearable. What should you do?

What do you think? Notice the question is:
What **should** you do? *not* What **would** you do?

3   What would you want the *shop* to do?

4   What *else* could the shop offer to do?

READING AND REACTING

A

1. Read the first paragraph again.
2. Now read paragraph 2 below.
3. What does the magazine advise you to do?
   (a) take the goods back immediately
   (b) write to say you are not happy with the goods
   (c) arrange for them to be collected

> Although there is no obligation on you to return the goods, it is best to take them back as soon as you discover the defect. If it is impractical for you to return to the shop at once, perhaps because you live a long way off, or because the goods are bulky, write to say that you are dissatisfied with the product and ask for collection arrangements to be made. Any unexplained or unreasonable delay will weaken your case.

B The writer uses very formal language above to say some simple things. First, which sentence in paragraph 2 above means:

1. You can't return to the shop.
2. You don't have to return the goods.

C Connect the formal words on the right from the text with their simple meanings on the left.

1. unhappy   *discover*
2. big   *defect*
3. fault   *bulky*
4. what you bought *dissatisfied*
5. find   *product*

D In paragraph 2 the writer uses single words to express complex ideas. Here are the ideas expressed as clauses. Can you find the single words with these meanings in paragraph 2 above?

1. something which you don't explain
2. something which is more than most people would accept or understand
3. the complaint which you are making

E Who should you complain to first?

1. the company that made the goods
2. the shop that sold the goods

Read the next paragraph and find out.

> Many people believe that the initial complaint about faulty goods should be made to the manufacturer. This is not the case. Your contract is with the retailer, the party who sold you the goods, and so it is to him that your complaint should be made.

F What does it mean - *the party* - in the paragraph above?

G Look at the heading and subheading of the next section:

HOW TO COMPLAIN
Make your complaint to the right person

Exam Work

Text Type, Audience and Reader's Purpose

As you read this text think about:

1. where the text has come from;
2. who it has been written for;
3. why someone would read the text.

Study Tip

Break down long words into sections by taking off the first part – the prefix – and the last part – the suffix or ending. So: *unwearable* = un-wear-able.

Try to recognise the middle of the word and then decide what extra meaning the prefix and suffix or ending gives. Prefixes often make words negative.

Who do you think is *the right person*?
Choose one of these people and then read the paragraph to check what the magazine advises.

1. the manager of the shop
2. the manager of the department which sold the goods
3. the assistant who sold you the goods
4. the assistant manager
5. the person in charge

> It is always a good idea to ask for the manager in a shop or the departmental manager in a large store. In asking for a person in authority you also show that you mean business right from the start. Don't be fobbed off with the common response that the manager is 'in a meeting' or 'away'. Insist that someone must have been left in charge and that you'll see that person. Failing that, register your complaint with the assistant and make an appointment to call back and see the manager at a mutually convenient time.

H Put these actions in the order the magazine suggests:
(a) make an appointment to see the manager
(b) register your complaint with the assistant
(c) ask to see the manager
(d) ask to see the person in charge

I Why should you...

1. ask to see the manager?
2. insist someone must have been left in charge?
3. register your complaint with the assistant?

J The next paragraph continues with advice on How to Complain.
Put some of the words from the paragraph below in two columns:

things you should do or be   **things you shouldn't do or be.**

Be polite but firm
When making your complaint it is important that you adopt the right tone. The last thing you want to do is antagonise the person you are dealing with. You should try to be polite but firm and give a generally businesslike impression. Maintain this approach and avoid having a row.

antagonise   give a businesslike impression   be polite
be firm   have a row   maintain this approach

Study Tip

We have seen before how important it is to recognise the *purpose* of a sentence or phrase. As you are reading this kind of text, keep thinking:
Is the writer saying this is a *good thing* or a *bad thing*?
Is this a positive point or a negative one?

K The next paragraph has a *subheading*, as in **G** above.
Read the paragraph and then decide which is the best subheading from the list below:

1 Know what you want
2 Return faulty products to the seller
3 Make sure you get what you want
4 Ask for a refund

> It is remarkable how many people return faulty products to the seller not having the faintest idea what they want to happen. Do you want a full refund, a repair, a credit note or an exchange? You may not get what you want but you should decide beforehand.

L The paragraph above suggests four things the shop might offer.
Match the words from the text on the left with their meanings on the right.

1	refund	a good one of the same type
2	repair	your money back
3	credit note	the fault made good
4	exchange	a letter saying you can get something there in the future of the same value

M What exactly is the *legal requirement* on the customer according to the next paragraph? Tick the correct one.

1 You must have a receipt. ☐
2 You must have paid by cheque or credit card. ☐
3 An assistant must remember serving you. ☐
4 Someone must have seen you buy the goods. ☐
5 You must have something to prove you bought the goods. ☐
6 The name of the shop must be on the goods. ☐

Take a receipt

Wherever possible try to take your receipt back with the goods. A receipt can prove that the goods were bought from a particular shop or store. A shop will want to make sure that the goods were bought there before considering your complaint. However, you are not legally obliged to show a receipt. You may have some other proof of purchase: for example, you may have a cheque stub or credit card voucher, or a particular trader's name may be stitched or stamped on to the product or an assistant may remember you, or you may have had someone with you when you bought the goods.

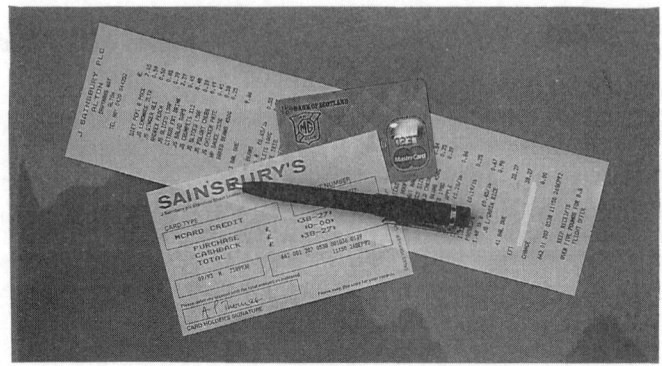

> **Study Tip**
>
> Use paragraph and section headings to help you to understand the contents of a paragraph.
>
> If there is no heading, think while you are reading:
>
> What could be the heading of this paragraph?
>
> You may be asked in the examination to give a heading to a section of text.

N A receipt shows:

the money you paid for something
the date you purchased it
the name of the shop

What information do these things show:

1   a cheque stub
2   a credit card voucher

O   Now read the whole text on pages 99–100 and answer the questions that go with it. For those with a **With Answers** edition, the Key to this unit begins on page 116.

In this Unit

...you have learned how to improve your skills in reading in the following areas:

understanding the main point of a paragraph;
using paragraph headings and subheadings to help with understanding;
understanding formal equivalents of common informal words and phrases;
breaking down long words into recognisable sections.

UNIT 11 An English-Speaking World

BACKGROUND BUILDING

The text you are going to read is from a book called *The Story of English*.

1 What information would you expect to find in a book with this title? Think of three kinds of information.

2 Now try to answer the questions in these two quizzes. They will start you thinking about the things in the text.

Quiz 1: The World

1 What is the population of the Earth?
   (a) 1 million   (b) 10 million   (c) 100 million   (d) 1000 million
   (e) more than 1000 million

2 How many countries are members of the United Nations?
   (a) 50   (b) 100   (c) 150   (d) 200   (e) more than 200

3 How many languages are there in the world?
   (a) 50   (b) 500   (c) 1000   (d) 2000   (e) more than 2000

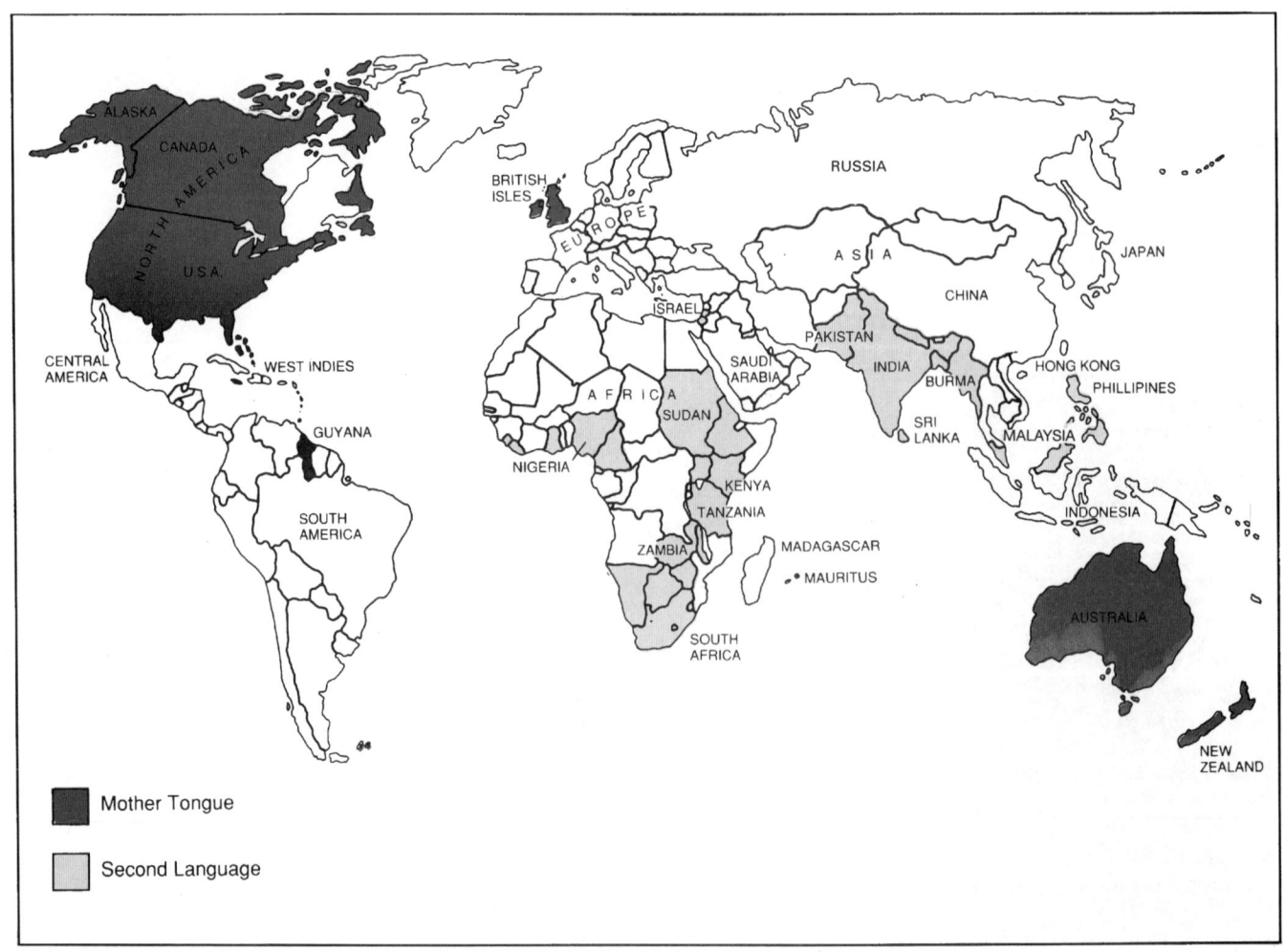

Quiz 2: The English Language

1. How many people speak English in the world?
   (a) 10 million (b) 50 million (c) 100 million (d) 1000 million
   (e) more than 1000 million

2. How old is the English language?
   (a) 500 years (b) 1000 years (c) 1500 years (d) 2000 years
   (e) more than 2000 years

3. How many words are there in the English language?
   (a) 10,000 (b) 50,000 (c) 100,000 (d) 1 million (e) more than 1 million

4. True or False?
   (a) Over 50% of the world's technical and scientific magazines are in English.
   (b) Over three-quarters of the information stored in the world's computers is in English.
   (c) Seventy-five per cent of the world's mail is in English.
   (d) Over 50% of the world's business deals are in English.

READING AND REACTING

A In paragraph 1 of the text the basic information is very simple, but the way it is written makes the paragraph very complicated. Read the first sentence:

> On 5 September 1977, the American spacecraft Voyager One blasted off on its historic mission to Jupiter and beyond.

A simpler way of saying this would be:

> On 5 September 1977, the American spaceship (called Voyager One) took off on its important journey to the planets.

So which word in the original sentence means:

1. important
2. journey
3. took off
4. What do you think Jupiter is?

B Read the second sentence:

> On board, the scientists, who knew that Voyager would one day spin through distant star systems, had installed a recorded greeting from the people of the planet Earth.

A simpler way of saying this is:

> The scientists had put a message from the people of the world on the spaceship because they knew it would one day travel to places a very long way away.

So what do these words mean from the original sentence?

1. on board
2. install
3. recorded greeting
4. the planet Earth
5. distant

Study Tip

This first sentence is difficult to read because the subject noun phrase is very long: *The American spacecraft Voyager One*.

Find the 'head word' in a long noun phrase – in this case *spacecraft*.

It is essential that you understand this head word. You don't always have to understand the adjectives or other words which come before or after it: *the American... Voyager One*.

Study Tip

Ignore long relative clauses like this one in the second sentence during the first reading. Find the *subject* and jump forward until you find the *verb* and then jump forward again until you find the *object*. This sentence becomes: *The scientists had installed a recorded greeting*.

Study Tip

Ignore non-finite clauses at the beginning of sentences during the first reading.

Ignore extra clauses after the object during the first reading.

The sentence then becomes:
The gold-plated disc
plays a statement.

If you apply the **Study Tip** for **A** on page 47 and find the head word, the sentence then becomes:
The disc plays a statement.
...which is very easy

C Read these simple statements. Then read the next sentence and decide if they are true (T) or false (F).

1 There was a statement and a message. _____
2 The message was in English. _____
3 The statement was in English. _____
4 The statement came before the message. _____
5 The statement and the message were on a cassette. _____
6 The statement was from the Secretary-General of the United States. _____
7 He was speaking for the members of the U.N. _____

Preceding a brief message in fifty-five different languages for the people of outer space, the gold-plated disc plays a statement, from the Secretary-General of the United Nations, an Austrian named Kurt Waldheim, speaking on behalf of 147 member states - in English.

Note:
This sentence is difficult to understand at first because:

    it begins with a non-finite clause: *Preceding...*
    it ends with a long set of extra clauses,
    giving more information about the object: *a statement...*

D Read the next two paragraphs. Complete the table.

DATE	NUMBER OF ENGLISH SPEAKERS
2000 years ago	
	as many as speak Cherokee
end of 16th C.	
the present	

    The rise in English is a remarkable story. When Julius Caesar landed in Britain nearly two thousand years ago, English did not exist. Five hundred years later, *Englisc*, incomprehensible to modern ears, was probably spoken by about as few people as currently speak Cherokee - and with about as little influence. Nearly a thousand years later, at the end of the sixteenth century, when William Shakespeare was in his prime, English was the native speech of between five and six million Englishmen and it was, in the words of a contemporary, 'of small reach, it stretches no further than this island of ours, no, not there over all'.

    Four hundred years later, the contrast is extraordinary. Between 1600 and the present, in armies, navies, companies and expeditions, the speakers of English - including Scots, Irish, Welsh, American and many more - travelled into every corner of the globe, carrying their language and culture with them. Today, English is used by at least 750 million people, and barely half of those speak it as a mother tongue. Some estimates have put that figure closer to one billion. Whatever the total, English at the end of the twentieth century is more widely scattered, more widely spoken and written, than any other language has ever been. It has become the language of the planet, the first truly global language.

56 Improving Your Reading

> **Study Tip**
>
> You must separate information you *need* to answer a question and information you *don't* need.
>
> If you are asked about dates and numbers of people, look just for that information, underline it when you find it and ignore the rest if you don't understand.

E There are large parts of the text above which do not help you complete the table. These are extra pieces of information or comments on the information, not *dates/times* or *numbers of* English *speakers*.

Tick the information that helped you to complete the table:

1. When Julius Caesar landed in Britain _____
2. English did not exist _____
3. incomprehensible to modern ears _____
4. and with about as little influence _____
5. Nearly a thousand years later _____
6. when William Shakespeare was in his prime _____
7. Between 1600 and the present, in armies, navies, companies and expeditions, the speakers of English – including Scots, Irish, Welsh, American and many more – travelled into every corner of the globe, carrying their language and culture with them. _____
8. Whatever the total, English at the end of the twentieth century is more widely scattered, more widely spoken and written, than any other language has ever been. It has become *the* language of the planet, the first truly global language. _____

F Look back at the two paragraphs above and find the answers to these questions.

1. What was the name for English in Julius Caesar's time?
2. How did English spread around the world in the last four hundred years?
3. Why does the text say English is **the** *language of the planet*?

G These words from the text are about language.

    native speech   mother tongue   incomprehensible speech   speakers

1. *native* commonly means 'a person born in a particular country' ...but what does it mean here?
2. *tongue* commonly means 'the organ in your mouth used for talking, tasting, licking' ...but what does it mean here?
3. *mother* commonly means 'the person who bore you' ...but what does it mean here?
4. *comprehend* means 'understand' ...so what does *incomprehensible* mean?
5. *speech* has three common meanings:
       'talk in public'   'power of speaking'   'a particular language'
    Which does it mean in this case?
6. *speaker* has three common meanings:
       'person who speaks a particular language'
       'person who is making a speech, or simply talking'
       'part of a hi-fi which produces the sounds'
    Which does it mean in this case?

H The next paragraph is about the *statistics* of English. So what do you expect to find in this paragraph? Tick one:

    dates   numbers   times   people

Improving Your Reading 57

I In the left-hand column below are some of the numbers from the next paragraph. In the right-hand column are what the numbers represent in this paragraph, but they are jumbled up.

1   Before you read the paragraph, try to guess what each number represents.

2700	words in English
one million	words in French
185,000	words in German
100,000	people who use English as a mother tongue
350 million	languages in the world

2   Now read the paragraph and check your guesses.

> The statistics are astonishing. Of all the world's languages (which now number some 2700), it is arguably the richest in vocabulary. The *Oxford English Dictionary* lists about 500,000 words; and a further half million technical and scientific terms remain uncatalogued. According to traditional estimates, neighbouring German has a vocabulary of about 185,000 words and French fewer than 100,000. About 350 million people use the English vocabulary as a mother tongue: about one-tenth of the world's population.

J   Look at the last sentence again...from *About 350*...
Answer these questions:

1   How many people *exactly* speak English as a mother tongue?
    (a) more than 350 million   (b) less than 350 million   (c) we don't know
2   What, according to this sentence, is the population of the world?
    (a) 35 million   (b) 350 million   (c) 3500 million   (d) 35,000 million

K   We are talking here about *proportion* which can be given as a *fraction* or a *percentage*.

1   Match the fractions, percentages and words below.

FRACTIONS	PERCENTAGES	WORDS
1/4	50%	a tenth
1/2	75%	a third
3/4	33.3%	three quarters
1/10	10%	a quarter
1/3	25%	half

2   Now read the final section and use the information about proportion to organise the things below. Which item has the largest proportion in English. Put 1 by the largest. Then find the second largest, the third largest, etc.

mail _____
information stored on computer _____
technical and scientific periodicals _____
business deals in Europe _____

Three-quarters of the world's mail, and its telexes and cables, are in English. So are more than half the world's technical and scientific periodicals: it is the language of technology from Silicon Valley to Shanghai. English is the medium for 80 per cent of the information stored in the world's computers. Nearly half of all business deals in Europe are conducted in English. Five of the largest broadcasting companies in the world transmit in English to audiences that regularly exceed one hundred million.

3   Which of the items in **K**2 above do you think is most important for the future of English?

L   To complete 2 in **K** you needed to understand proportion and extra words like **nearly** = 'less than' and **exceed** = 'more than'. These extra words change the proportion slightly.

Put the words below into the correct columns. Two of the words will not fit into either column. Can you find them and explain why?

LESS THAN	MORE THAN

barely   over   in excess of   above   nearly   almost
about   approximately

M   Read the text on pages 100–101 and do the quizzes again on pages 54–55. Then answer the questions that go with the text.
For those with a **With Answers** edition, the Key to this unit begins on page 118.

In this Unit

...you have learned how to improve your skills in reading in the following areas:

decoding complex sentences into subject, verb and object finding head words in noun phrases;
dealing with non-defining relative clauses;
recognising important information in a paragraph.

Improving Your Reading   59

UNIT 12 Coming to the UK

BACKGROUND BUILDING

1 What is the connection between all these items?

opium, heroin, morphine, cocaine;
counterfeit coins;
firearms, flick knives;
horror comics, indecent or obscene books, magazines, films;
meat and poultry;
CB radios;
plants, certain fish, most animals and all birds whether alive or dead.

2 The text you are going to read is from a British Government leaflet entitled:

> **BRINGING YOUR BELONGINGS TO THE UNITED KINGDOM**

(a) What are *belongings*?
(b) When do people bring their belongings to the United Kingdom?
(c) What countries are called, together, the United Kingdom?

3 You arrive in Britain and a British Customs officer asks you:

> Have you got anything to declare?

You answer:

> Yes, officer, _____

Complete the sentence with something suitable.

READING AND REACTING

A In **Background Building** we considered reasons for bringing your belongings to the UK. The leaflet you are going to read gives information for people in this position.

60 Improving Your Reading

Exam Work

When you have worked out the text type, you can usually guess the reader's purpose in reading it. For example, this text is from a government leaflet about bringing your belongings to the UK. This information helps you to work out why someone would read the text. Choose from A – D below:

A to check the cost of sending goods to the UK
B to check the law about immigration to the UK
C to check the law about bringing personal goods into the UK
D to find out the best way of sending goods to the UK

If you are bringing your belongings to the UK, what questions would you want the leaflet to answer? Can you think of at least three? (See the bottom of the page if you can't think of any!)

B When you read leaflets like this, you do not need to read every section – only the sections which concern you. You need to decide which sections to read – and the leaflet has a special section to help you do this:

Which Sections Apply to You

1 Choose a reason for bringing your belongings which might really apply to you, from the list below.
   (a) coming for a holiday
   (b) coming to study
   (c) coming to live for a short time
   (d) coming back to live in the UK (you used to live here before)
   (e) coming to buy a house – as a second home
2 Now read this introductory section. Which sections of the leaflet should *you* read? Tick the sections below as you read:

   Section 1 _____ 2 _____ 3 _____ 4 _____ 5 _____

Which Sections Apply to You

All travellers should read Section 1.
If you are visiting the UK (or coming here as a student), read Section 2.
If you are moving, or returning, to the UK, read Section 3.
If you are setting up a secondary home in the UK or giving up a secondary home abroad, read Section 4.
If you have belongings originally obtained in the UK, or the EC, read Section 5.

C For most people studying this book, the important part will be Section 1 because you would be a *traveller* and Section 2 because you would be *visiting*, or *coming here as a student*.

These are the sections we are going to study.

Questions:
  1 What exactly do I have to do?
  2 What do I have to declare?
  3 Do I have to pay tax on my belongings?
  4 How much do I have to pay?

Improving Your Reading 61

Study Tip

When you have to read official leaflets, write down first exactly what you want to find out.

Then check which sections will provide you with that information and read only those sections.

D Section 1 is entitled **General Information**

Here are the paragraph headings:

1 What is this notice about?
2 Duty-free allowances
3 Pets
4 Prohibited and restricted goods
5 Other Customs notices

Which paragraph will you check to find out:

1 how many cigarettes you can bring in?
2 whether you can bring your dog?
3 whether you can bring plant seeds?
4 how you can bring in your car?
5 the purpose of the leaflet?

E In most cases, Section 1 refers you to other sources to find the exact answers to your questions.

Read Section 1 below and make a note of where you must look for the exact information to answer questions 1 – 4 above:

1 cigarettes _____
2 dog _____
3 plant seeds _____
4 car _____

Exam Work

Matching Headings

You are going to read part of a government leaflet. Choose the most suitable heading from the list A – H for each space in the text 1 – 7. There is one extra heading which you do not need to use.

A Duty-free allowances
B General information
C Passport and visa requirements
D Information all travellers need to know
E Other Customs notices
F Pets
G Prohibited and restricted goods
H What is this notice about?

| 1 |
| 2 |

(See Section 2 for the meaning of certain words)

| 3 |

It tells you about bringing your belongings through UK Customs and which of these may be imported free of duty and tax.

| 4 |

In addition to the reliefs in Section 4 to 7, you can have the allowances for alcoholic drinks, tobacco products, perfume and toilet water and other goods (popularly known as 'duty frees'). These are listed in our Notice 1 and are shown on the display posters in the baggage halls.

If you are moving your home to the UK from within the EC, you may qualify for an extra (though limited) amount of alcoholic drink and tobacco products as explained in paragraph 22.

| 5 |

Your pet can count as part of your belongings, but you must see paragraph 4 about the restrictions on importing live animals, fish and birds. You must fill in a Form C3 for each pet.

| 6 |

Don't be tempted to import illegally any prohibited or restricted goods. These are listed in our Notice 2.

62 Improving Your Reading

| 7 | |

You may need to look at other Customs notices if you are:
- bringing in a private motor vehicle – see Notice 3A;
- bringing in a pleasure craft – see Notice 8 or 8A;
- moving to the UK on marriage – see Notice 4;
- bringing in inherited goods – see Notice 368;
- bringing in antiques – see Notice 362.

Study Tip

Official and legal texts often use unfamiliar head words to cover familiar items – such as *motor vehicle* for *car, motorcycle, van*. Don't panic if you meet one of these words. Examples later in the text often make it clear what the head word covers.

F The words below are not actually mentioned in the text. What word or phrase does the text use to cover these words?

Example: whisky   *alcoholic drinks*

1 cigarettes _____
2 dogs _____
3 personal possessions _____
4 car _____
5 drugs _____

G 'May' and 'can' have several meanings depending on context.
In this text, they mean either: (a) is/are allowed *or* (b) is/are possible

1 Mark each appearance of these words in the text above (a) or (b).
2 Discuss your answers with the people near you.

Study Tip

Look very carefully at modals in this kind of official text. They are carefully chosen to express a particular idea.

H How did the text express the underlined ideas? Can you remember the exact words used?

1 You can <u>bring in</u> some goods ....
2 <u>without paying anything</u>.
3 These allowances are <u>extra</u> ....
4 to the <u>allowances</u> in Sections 4 to 7.
5 If you are moving from <u>another EC country</u>
6 you may <u>be able to get</u> an extra allowance.
7 Your pet can <u>be considered</u> part of your belongings
8 Don't <u>try</u> to import illegally ....
9 any goods which are <u>not allowed</u> ...
10 or <u>where the import is controlled</u>.
11 See other notices about <u>boats</u> ...
12 <u>things which you got from dead relatives</u> ...
13 or <u>very old things</u>.

I Many people studying this book will come to the UK as a visitor or a student. These people must read Section 2. Imagine:

> You are a student intending to study in the UK for six months. You do not have any presents, but you have brought personal belongings including sheets and blankets, books you will need at the school and some things for your accommodation.

1 Can you take all of these things into the UK?
2 What do you have to do at UK Customs?

Improving Your Reading 63

2. Visiting the UK

For everyone who usually lives outside the UK and does not intend to move their normal home to the UK. Students whose normal home is outside the UK count as visitors.

D Rules of the relief

As a visitor your belongings can be free of duty and tax and need not be declared to the Customs so long as:

- all belongings are brought in with you and are for your use alone;
and
- they are kept in the UK for no more than 6 months in a 12-month period;
and
- you do NOT sell, lend, hire out or otherwise dispose of them in the UK;
and
- they are exported either:
  - when you leave the UK; or
  - before they have been in the UK for more than 6 months, WHICHEVER HAPPENS FIRST.

For private motor vehicles, see Notice 3A.

E Students

Students who usually live outside the UK can temporarily import belongings under the relief in paragraph D.

In addition, if you are on a full-time course of study at a school, college or university, you can permanently import, free of duty and tax, for your own personal use, your:

- clothing and household linen;
and
- articles for use in your studies;
and
- household effects for furnishing your rooms.

These items must be declared as explained in paragraph 10.

64 Improving Your Reading

J Which of the following changes will affect the situation?
Answer Yes or No and be prepared to quote the relevant regulation.

Example: If your belongings do not accompany you
   Yes; it says *so long as they are brought in with you*

1 if you intend to sell something whilst in the UK
   _____

2 if you stay more than 6 months
   _____

3 if you are on a part-time course of study
   _____

K What do they mean?

1 What is the opposite of *for your use only*?
2 Why does the text say *a 12-month period* not *a year*?
3 How could you *otherwise dispose of belongings*?
4 How would you *export them when you leave the* UK (in simple language)?
5 *Whichever happens first*: What exactly is your choice?
   You can _____ or _____
6 What is the opposite of *temporarily* (it's in the next paragraph)?

L How many items can you think of for each of the final categories in the text?

1 clothing and household linen
2 articles for use in your studies
3 household effects for furnishing your rooms

M Read the full text again on pages 102–103 and answer the questions that go with it.
For those with a **With Answer** edition, the Key to this unit begins on page 120.

Study Tip

Official and legal texts use very carefully chosen language. They do this because there could be extremely serious consequences of someone misunderstanding them. As a student reading these texts, you must look very carefully at every word and think: Why have they said it that way? For example, *a year = 12 months* in general conversation, but a year could suggest *a period from January to December*, not any period of 12 months.

In this Unit

...you have learned how to improve your skills in reading in the following areas:
finding your way through official leaflets;
recognising formal head words and their hyponyms;
interpreting legalistic language.

Improving Your Reading 65

Practice Test

Part 1

You are going to read a government leaflet about UK Customs. Choose the most suitable heading from the list **A – J** for each part (**1 – 8**) of the text. There is one extra heading which you do not need to use. There is an example at the beginning (**0**).

A	A list of your belongings
B	Before you arrive
C	How to declare
D	How to go through Customs
E	Opening luggage
F	Paying duty and tax
G	Prohibited and restricted goods
H	Seeing our officer
I	What to declare
J	When you arrive at Customs

0	D

(See Section 2 for the meanings of certain words.)

1	

Before you arrive you should know:
- which belongings you must declare to Customs (paragraph 9 explains this);
- which goods are prohibited or restricted (paragraph 4 gives examples).

2	

Most ports and airports use a system of Red and Green Channels.
Red means you have something to declare, and Green means you have nothing to declare.

Where the Red/Green system is in use, you must do as the large public notice tells you. When the Red/Green system is not in use, or if you go through the Red Channel, you will meet one of our officers. The officers want to be as quick and helpful as possible. It will help everyone if you do as this notice tells you.

3	

Our officer will ask if you have anything to 'declare'.

Improving Your Reading 67

4

You should declare anything you have which:
- this notice or another Customs notice tells you to declare

and
- is more than the duty and tax-free allowances shown both in our Notice 1 and on the large display notices in the baggage halls.

If you have nothing to declare, go through the Green Channel or tell our officer if you are asked.

NOTE: IF YOU ARE UNSURE, DECLARE THE GOODS.

5

If you bring your belongings in with you, simply tell the officer.

If you send them in, you must fill in and sign a Customs Form C3 and attach to it a detailed packing list.

Most people employ a shipping agent to look after their belongings if they cannot deal in person with Customs.

You should get Form C3 from your shipping agent. Otherwise, contact us at the address on the inside of the front cover.

6

A list of belongings you wish to declare can be helpful, but our officer may still want to question you or examine your luggage.

7

Under the law, you must open, unpack and repack your luggage if the officer asks you. Pack the belongings to be declared in a place you can easily get at.

8

You must pay duty and tax on items which do not fulfil all the rules of relief. Also, we may require a deposit of duty and tax until you prove all the rules of relief are fulfilled.

Part 2

You are going to read an extract from a novel. For Questions **9 – 16**, choose the correct answer **A**, **B**, **C** or **D**.

My part in the affair started on September 18th, when my chief sent for me and told me he was transferring me to Saxmere on the east coast. He was sorry about it, he said, but I was the only one with the necessary technical qualifications for the particular work they had on hand. No, he couldn't give me any details; they were an odd lot down there, and shut themselves up behind barbed wire at the slightest provocation. The place had been a radar experimental station a few years back, but this was finished, and any experiments that were going on now were of an entirely different nature, something to do with vibrations and the pitch of sound.

'I'll be perfectly frank with you,' said my chief, removing his horn-rimmed spectacles and waving them in the air apologetically. 'The fact is that James Maclean is a very old friend of mine. We were at Cambridge together and I saw a lot of him then and afterwards, but our paths diverged, and he tied himself up in experimental work of a rather dubious nature. Lost the government a lot of money, and didn't do his own reputation much good either. I gather that's forgotten, and he's been reinstated down at Saxmere with his own hand-picked team of experts and a government grant. They're stuck for an electronics engineer – which is where you come in. Maclean has sent me an S.O.S. for someone I can vouch for personally – in other words, he wants a chap who won't talk. You'd do me a personal favour if you went.'

Put like this, there was little I could do but accept. It was a damned nuisance all the same. The last thing in the world I wanted to do was to leave Associated Electronics Ltd. and its unique facilities for research, and drift off to the east coast to work for someone who had blotted his copybook once and might do so again.

'When do you want me to go?' I asked.

The chief looked more apologetic than ever.

'As soon as you can make it. The day after tomorrow? I'm really very sorry, Saunders. With any luck you'll be back by Christmas. I've told Maclean I'm lending you to him for this particular project only. No question of a long-term transfer. You're too valuable here.'

9 The story is probably going to be
- **A** a love story.
- **B** a war story.
- **C** a science fiction story.
- **D** a western.

10 The writer was being transferred to Saxmere because
- **A** it was an experimental radar station.
- **B** his chief did not want him anymore
- **C** he couldn't talk.
- **D** they urgently needed an electronics engineer.

11 The writer's chief
- **A** knew what was happening at Saxmere.
- **B** had a vague idea what was happening at Saxmere.
- **C** had no idea what was happening at Saxmere.
- **D** thought they were doing something odd at Saxmere.

12 Maclean was conducting experiments into
- **A** radar.
- **B** nature.
- **C** sound.
- **D** electronics.

13 The chief wanted to help Maclean because
- **A** they had been at Cambridge together.
- **B** he had lost a lot of money.
- **C** they were old friends.
- **D** he felt sorry for him.

14 James Maclean's career
  A had started well but had declined.
  B had started badly but had improved.
  C had never gone very well.
  D had suffered a temporary set-back.

15 The writer didn't want to go to Saxmere because
  A it was on the east coast.
  B he didn't have any details of the job.
  C he didn't like Maclean.
  D he wanted to stay at Associated Electronics.

16 The chief wanted the writer to go
  A in two days' time.
  B immediately.
  C before Christmas.
  D as soon as he had completed his work.

Part 3

You are going to read a newspaper article about the assassination of Rajiv Gandhi. Eight sentences have been removed from the article. Choose from the sentences **A – I** the one which fits each gap (**17 – 23**). There is one extra sentence which you do not need to use. There is an example at the beginning (**0**).

Rural Tamil Nadu in southern India looks peaceful enough, even though this is India's most violent election campaign ever. White swans slowly flap across the sun-scorched rice fields which are being readied for planting in July when the rains come.

But at the beginning of last week an air of expectancy suddenly pervaded this pastoral atmosphere. **0** **D** From one small village to another, wherever his motorcade was expected to stop, the red carpet was being rolled out.

The villagers of Sriperumbudur had not experienced such excitement since Gandhi last visited them in 1987. **17** Not everyone felt happy about it, however. The local police forces, responsible for his security, were uneasy about crowd control in such a remote spot as Sriperumbudur at night. They were worried that the Tamil Tigers were somehow still active in this region. **18**

The final two hours of Gandhi's life started at 8.30 p.m. when his aircraft finally touched down at the old Madras airport, an hour behind schedule because of mechanical problems. Perhaps because of confusion over his arrival time, airport security was already pretty relaxed. **19**

Gandhi's bullet-proof white Ambassador took its place near the front of a convoy of about 30 vehicles, including police vans.

It was already dark. **20**

At Sriperumbudur's entrance Gandhi got down and demonstrated his casualness by allowing himself to be surrounded by a dense crowd of well-wishers. **21**

Three or four minutes later he climbed back into his car for the short run to the election meeting, where his murderer was already waiting. **22**

The state president had gone on to the stage and was lining up the candidates

Gandhi would introduce to the audience. 23 [   ] It is clear that Gandhi's murderer had somehow avoided any security. She walked through the barricade until she was just feet away from her target.

A   After a wash, Gandhi entered the airport lounge, and then moved out to his car.
B   Gandhi's motorcade was due in at 9 p.m.
C   India is the largest democracy in the world.
D   Rajiv Gandhi, India's former prime minister, was on the campaign trail in Tamil Nadu.
E   Rajiv started walking down the red carpet.
F   The Tigers are the most hard-line of all the Tamil militant groups.
G   The security was virtually non-existent.
H   There, he got out of the car again and started to walk the last 25 yards to the platform.
I   The convoy bumped and honked through the confusion of the suburbs out into the Tamil Nadu countryside.

Part 4

You are going to read some information for vehicle owners in the UK.
For Questions **24 – 35**, choose from the sections **A – J** the one you need to read in each case. Some of the sections may be chosen more than once. When more than one answer is required, these may be given in any order. There is an example at the beginning (**0**).
For Questions **34** and **35**, choose the correct answer **A, B, C** or **D**.

Which section or sections should you read if…

you buy a new car from a dealer?	**0** A
you buy a car without a tax disc from a friend?	**24** [ ] **25** [ ]
your tax disc is stolen?	**26** [ ] **27** [ ]
you don't receive a reminder to pay Vehicle Excise Duty?	**28** [ ]
you move house?	**29** [ ]
you scrap a car yourself?	**30** [ ]
you sell your car to a garage?	**31** [ ]
you take your car with you on a two-year contract abroad?	**32** [ ]
you want to keep the registration number of a previous car?	**33** [ ]

34 Where has this text come from?
   A a consumer magazine
   B a manual for car drivers
   C a government leaflet
   D a magazine for car dealers

35 Why would someone read this leaflet?
   A if they had just bought or sold a vehicle
   B if their vehicle had been stolen
   C if they needed to register a vehicle
   D any of the above

Services we provide

Vehicles

A

When you acquire a brand new vehicle the dealer will usually arrange for it to be registered for you through a Vehicle Registration Office (VRO) on form V55. You should ensure that they enter your name, address and postcode correctly and clearly on the form. You can also apply to the VRO yourself – addresses can be found in leaflet V100 (from Post Offices) or in some telephone directories under **Transport – Department of**. The VRO will allocate a registration number and arrange for the vehicle Registration Document (V5) – (log book) to be posted to you.

B

When you acquire a used vehicle the previous keeper should give you the Registration Document (V5). You should complete the changes section on the reverse of the V5 to confirm acquisition and send it to DVLC, Swansea, SA99 1AR. If you buy a vehicle without a Registration Document you can apply for one on form V62 available from Post Offices. We will issue a Registration Document. If you also need to license the vehicle, you can do so at a Post Office (See **Section H**). The Post Office will then send us your completed V5 or V62 so that we can send you a new Registration Document.

C

When you sell your vehicle you should complete the lower, tear-off portion of the Registration Document and send it to DVLC, Swansea, SA99 1AR. It is **your** responsibility to do this, even when you sell to a garage. The rest of the form should be given to the purchaser to complete and send in.

D

If you change your name/address or vehicle details, complete the relevant section on the reverse of the Registration Document and send it to DVLC, Swansea, SA99 1AR. We will issue a replacement Registration Document free of charge.

E

If you scrap your vehicle complete the lower, tear-off part of the Registration Document and send it to DVLC, Swansea, SA99 1AR, unless you **personally** break up the vehicle. The rest of the Registration Document should be given to the new keeper, for example, the insurance company or scrap dealer. If you have broken up the vehicle, complete the notification of scrapping on the reverse of the

Registration Document and send it to DVLC, Swansea, SA99 1AR. This will enable us to prevent a stolen vehicle assuming its identity. If you wish to retain the registration mark displayed on the vehicle make sure you make arrangements to transfer the mark **before** you dispose of the vehicle. You may otherwise lose the right to display it. (See leaflet V317 for more information on the transfer of registration marks.)

F

If you export your vehicle for more than 12 months, we issue certificates of export to enable you to register your vehicle abroad. Complete the notification of export section on the reverse of the Registration Document and apply at a VRO for the certificate (or send to DVLC).

G

If your Registration Document is lost or stolen, complete form V62 and send it to DVLC, Swansea, SA99 1AR. We will issue a new Registration Document. If you need the document to relicense your vehicle you can complete form V62 at the Post Office when you apply for a tax disc. (See below.)

H

You can pay Vehicle Excise Duty (VED) at any of 4000 licensing Post Offices. If you are recorded as the vehicle keeper we will send you a renewal reminder form V11 (V11W in Wales) which is also your application to renew the VED licence.

If you do not receive a reminder you can still apply by completing form V10 available at Post Offices. A Welsh version of the form (V10W) is available at Welsh Post Offices. Heavy Goods Vehicles keepers will need to apply to the VRO using a form V85.

Your application (V11 or V10) must be accompanied by the correct payment, a valid certificate of insurance and, where appropriate, MOT certificate. Applications on form V10 should be accompanied by the Registration Document, if available, or completed form V62.

I

If your tax disc is lost or stolen VRO's will issue, over the counter, a **duplicate VED disc** when you complete form V20, accompanied by the Registration Document (form V62 if V5 is not available) and appropriate fee. If you are not the registered keeper of the vehicle the VRO will request additional details to verify your application. You might initially be issued with a temporary tax disc.

J

If you no longer intend to keep or use your vehicle on the road, or wish to sell it, you can surrender the tax disc to claim a refund for each **unexpired** whole month. Send a completed form V14 (available from Post Offices) with the tax disc to DVLC, Swansea, SA99 1AL.

If you do not have a VED disc, e.g. if your vehicle has been stolen or the disc lost, send a completed form V33 (available from VRO's) to DVLC, Swansea, SA99 1AL.

CAMBRIDGE
EXAMINATIONS, CERTIFICATES AND DIPLOMAS
ENGLISH AS A FOREIGN LANGUAGE

University of Cambridge
Local Examinations Syndicate
International Examinations

For Supervisor's use only

Shade here if the candidate is ABSENT or has WITHDRAWN

Examination Details	9999/01	99/D99
Examination Title	First Certificate in English	
Centre/Candidate No.	AA999/9999	
Candidate Name	A.N. EXAMPLE	

• Sign here if the details above are correct

• Tell the Supervisor now if the details above are not correct

Candidate Answer Sheet: FCE Paper 1 Reading

Use a pencil

Mark ONE letter for each question.

For example, if you think **B** is the right answer to the question, mark your answer sheet like this:

Change your answer like this:

FCE-1

© UCLES/K&J

DP999/99

SECTION 2 Improving Your Vocabulary

Unit 1 Mind that Child!

A Opposites

What is the opposite of each of the words in italics *in the context given*?
Example: Road accidents are a *major* cause of death. <u>minor</u>

1 The cyclist was *seriously* injured. _____
2 Most accidents happen on *residential* roads. _____
3 Sometimes the traffic on this road is *light*. _____
4 The child was acting *sensibly*. _____
5 That girl is very *immature* for her age. _____
6 *Children* are unable to judge speed. _____

B Roads and Traffic

What do we call...
Example: someone who drives a car <u>driver</u>

1 someone who walks _____
2 someone who rides a bicycle _____
3 when two cars hit each other _____
4 a place where you can cross the road _____
5 a place where roads meet _____
6 so many cars that you can't move _____
7 the place where pedestrians walk _____
8 an accident in which someone is killed _____
9 having no petrol _____
10 not working (a vehicle) _____

C Correct these sentences.

Explain your corrections.
Example: The child was damaged in the accident.
<u>injured not damaged – you can't damage a person</u>

1 You shouldn't cross when the traffic lamps are red.
   _____

2 A child is far more in risk than an adult.
   _____

3 The pedestrian was knocked off by a car.
   _____

4 I didn't see the driver's sign.
   _____

If you have a **With Answers** edition, check page 123 of the Key.

Unit 2 The Train Journey

A Opposites

What is the opposite of each of the words in italics *in the context given*?
Example: I met him *by chance*. <u>by arrangement</u>

1 The journey was *normal*. _____
2 It was a *dull* party. _____
3 It is difficult to see clearly *at dusk*. _____
4 He was tall and *lean*. _____
5 He speaks Italian *badly*. _____
6 There was a *goods* train in the station. _____
7 The government decided *in favour of* it. _____
8 There were *high* winds last night. _____

B Travel (1)

Can you complete the expression or give the verb to complete the chart?

VERBS	EXPRESSION
1 _fly_	go by air
2 _____	go by car
3 walk	go _____
4 ride (a horse)	go _____
5 _____	go by sea

C Travel (2)

What is the word or phrase for...
Example: an official on a train <u>a guard</u>

1 where people catch a train _____
2 where people wait for a train _____
3 what trains run on _____
4 a train that carries people _____
5 a train that carries things _____
6 a train that only stops at major stations _____
7 the separate parts of a passenger train _____
8 the separate parts of a goods train _____
9 the passage between two parts of a passenger train _____

D Correct these sentences.

Explain your corrections.

1 I'm tired from doing this job. _____
2 I have seen a good lot of him this week. _____
3 A government officer made a statement. _____
4 Meet John. He's a companion of mine at work. _____
5 'What's going here?' he shouted angrily. _____
6 You should give up your chair on a train for an elderly person. _____

If you have a **With Answers** edition, check pages 123–124 of the Key.

Unit 3 Green Lights

A Opposites

What is the opposite of the words in italics *in the context given*?
Example: Conventional bulbs use *more* electricity than fluorescent. <u>less</u>

1 Fluorescent bulbs work *in the same* way as tubes. _____
2 They *cost* you around £30 in their lifetime. _____
3 The light in the room was very *dim*. _____
4 These bulbs are good for *general* lighting. _____
5 This appliance is very *efficient*. _____

B Electricity in the Home

These words are all connected with electricity in the home. Can you explain what they are?

1 an electrician _____
2 the mains _____
3 an appliance _____
4 the lead _____
5 the fuse _____
6 the plug _____
7 a shock _____
8 a power cut _____
9 What is the difference between the two adjectives:
   electric   electrical?

C Talking about Products

Match the definitions and words with a line between them.

1 a product from a particular company   (a) cargo
2 a set of similar products   (b) consumer
3 one product in a set   (c) range
4 another name for products   (d) brand
5 a person who uses products   (e) producer
6 a person who makes products   (f) freight
7 products carried on a lorry or train   (g) model
8 products carried on a ship or plane   (h) goods

D Correct these sentences.

They use words and structures from the text.
Explain your corrections.

1 I'll buy the bigger one. It works cheaper than two small ones.
   _____

2 The fuse in this plug needs to replace.
   _____

3 The application form is closed with this letter.
   _____

Improving Your Vocabulary 77

4   The fire started in the concert.

5   I'm not sure of the price but they are nearly £10.

If you have a **With Answers** edition, check pages 124–125 of the Key.

Unit 4 Girls will be Girls

A Verbs and Prepositions

What can you...

1	look after?	(a)	a role, a job, a responsibility
2	believe in?	(b)	a baby, a child, a pet, a department
3	be aware of?	(c)	a discussion, a society, a plan
4	take on?	(d)	a problem, a noise, a movement
5	be involved in?	(e)	ideas, God, superstitions

Can you use the verbs + prepositions in sentences?

B Verbs and Nouns

What, in the article, can you...
Example: fight <u>*fires*</u>

1 mend _____
2 wear _____
3 inherit _____
4 commission _____
5 climb _____
6 do _____

Add some more nouns for each verb.
Now cover the verbs and try to remember them from the nouns.

C Talking about Education

What are these things? They are all connected with education in Britain.
Example: a pupil   <u>*a child at school*</u>

1 a subject _____
2 a curriculum _____
3 a syllabus _____
4 a college _____
5 an infant _____
6 a degree _____
7 a head _____
8 a principal _____
9 a term _____

If you have a **With Answers** edition, check page 125 of the Key.

78 Improving Your Vocabulary

Unit 5 Home Improvement Loans

A What's the difference?

Can you explain the difference between these pairs of words?
Example: tenant/owner
<u>a tenant rents a house/an owner has bought or is buying a house</u>

1 valuable/pricey

2 worthless/priceless

3 cost/value

4 insure/assure

5 office/branch

6 redundancy/dismissal

B Talking about Money

How many words can you think of which mean...

1 money you earn   2 money you pay   (Make two lists.)
3 Can you explain the difference between some of the words?

C Correct these sentences.

They use words and structures from the text. Explain your corrections.

1 It's time you leave. The train goes in 20 minutes.

2 This door must not be locked in case fire.

3 If you reply quickly we'll give you a 10% discount.
   Although, this offer closes on 31st July.

4 We strongly recommend you protecting your repayments.

5 I had enough money so I afforded it.

If you have a **With Answers** edition, check page 126 of the Key.

Unit 6 The Kennedy Conspiracy

A Politics (1)

In the box on the next page are some names for political leaders. Can you explain the differences between them by answering the questions underneath?

Prime Minister	President	Sultan	King	Governor
Mayor	Senator	Emperor	Dictator	

1 Which ones are elected?
2 Which ones are rulers of whole countries?
3 What is the political system called in their countries? For example, *monarchy*

B Politics (2)

Draw a line between the words connected with politics and their meanings.

1 vote — right or left side of politics
2 election — local government group
3 party — all the elected members
4 candidate — the ministers who advise the Prime Minister
5 stand for — to choose a candidate
6 parliament — the members who are against the government
7 opposition — a person who wants to represent an area
8 wing — a group of people with the same ideas
9 council — to be a candidate
10 cabinet — a time when people vote

C What comes next?

Many words in English affect the words which follow.
Example: I listened <u>to</u> the radio.

Follow the underlined words with something grammatically suitable.

1 The President said, 'I <u>wish I</u> _____
2 The secretary replied, 'Don't <u>worry</u> _____
3 The President had received <u>warnings</u> _____
4 Hubert Humphrey had <u>advised</u> _____
5 Kennedy was <u>determined</u> _____
6 The President <u>arrived</u> _____

D Where are they?

Where would you find...

1 spectators _____
2 audience _____
3 listeners _____
4 speakers _____
5 viewers _____
6 observers _____
7 onlookers _____
8 sightseers _____
9 watchmen _____
10 look-outs _____

If you have a **With Answers** edition, check page 127 of the Key.

Unit 7 The Disease Detectives

A Opposites

What is the opposite of each of the words in italics *in the context given*?

1 *Those who have a car* can use that. _____
2 *Some people* think it is a good idea. _____
3 *Nearly all* the results were good. _____
4 *One of the two men* was tall. _____
5 *More than* 500 people died. _____
6 Some of the victims *died*. _____
7 Many deaths happened *near* the pump. _____
8 He *regularly* goes to New York. _____
9 They *accepted* the idea. _____
10 Five years *later* cholera came. _____

B Disease (1)

Odd One Out
Circle the word which does not go with the other three.
Can you explain why it is different?

1 contract	catch	go down with	treat
2 get better	get well	get over	get
3 treat	tend	nurse	cure
4 medicine	pill	tablet	cough mixture
5 surgeon	doctor	physician	G.P.
6 ward	bed	cubicle	theatre
7 nurse	patient	sister	matron
8 examine	diagnose	prescribe	operate
9 brain	lungs	liver	heart

C Disease (2)

Can you say...? If not, why not?

1 The doctor examined my corpse.
2 'Flu is contagious.
3 The murdered buried the body.
4 He was in bad health when I last saw him.
5 I have suffered with asthma for years.
6 He fell ill just before his 80th birthday.
7 Insects can infect humans with some diseases.
8 He fought with the disease all his life.

D Verbs and Nouns

Can you change the seven verbs on the next page into nouns?

1. prescribe _____
2. treat _____
3. recover _____
4. improve _____
5. examine _____
6. break out _____
7. diagnose _____

If you have a **With Answers** edition, check pages 128–129 in the Key.

Unit 8 Fire!

A Opposites

What is the opposite of each of the words in italics *in the context given*?

1. Air-conditioning will sometimes pick up smoke from *one room*. _____
2. You should *keep that in mind*. _____
3. You should be *aware* of this problem. _____
4. We must get some *fresh* air into this room. _____
5. The hall was *completely* full of smoke. _____
6. He was so frightened he *panicked*. _____
7. The mask was *effective* against the smoke. _____
8. *Fold* the towel into a triangle. _____

B Talking about Fires

What do we call...

1. another word for burning _____
2. another phrase for burning (2 words) _____
3. to start a fire (3 words) _____
4. gas from burning materials _____
5. individual parts of a burning fire _____
6. to stop a fire (2 words) _____
7. a person whose job is to stop fires _____
8. a vehicle used to help stop fires _____

C Organising Phrases

Some phrases in texts organise the information and help you to follow the ideas of the writer.

1. What phrases would you expect to find later in the text if you read...
   The first thing is...
2. What sort of information would come before the phrase...
   In any case...
3. ...and what would come after?
4. What sort of information would come after phrases beginning...
   Here are (*a few tips, some things you can do*)
5. What would follow the phrase...
   The point is...

If you have a **With Answers** edition, check page 129 of the Key.

82 Improving Your Vocabulary

Unit 9 Death in the Family

A Prepositions (1): Place and Direction

We usually understand these quite easily. For this reason, they can often help us to understand the noun, or noun phrase, that follows.

1 Match the preposition with the noun or noun phrase by connecting them with a line. You can use the same preposition more than once.

on to	the bend
from	the stone steps
up	my lap
under	the overhanging branches
round	the terrace
into	his pocket
on	the long, sloping lane
	one of the pegs

2 Find out the correct answers from your colleagues, the teacher, or the text on page 88.
3 Can you get some idea of what the nouns or noun phrases must mean?
e.g. *up...the stone steps* so *steps* = something you can go up
Discuss with your colleagues.

B Prepositions (2)

Sometimes, prepositions do not have simple meanings of place or direction.
They go with verbs to make special meanings.
Can you explain the meanings of the underlined phrase in each sentence?

1 That's really <u>up to</u> Meg.
2 He said he'd <u>see to</u> all that.
3 He watched the car <u>move off</u>.
4 It was a long time since Fred had <u>been up to</u> playing with a ball.
5 He walked <u>in by</u> the French windows.
6 He went outside to <u>see</u> the vet <u>off</u>.

Look at your answers to 1 and 4 above. What's the different between:

(a) *It's not up to him.* (b) *He's not up to it.*

C Groups

Put the words below into groups. You decide how many groups, but you must be able to explain your grouping.

carpet	floor	window	branches	pine	trees
border	terrace	pocket	raincoat	steps	lane
bend	peg	grass	drive	drawing room	

If you have a **With Answers** edition, check pages 129–130 of the Key.

Improving Your Vocabulary 83

Unit 10 How to Complain

A Talking about Shopping

What do we call...

1 a person who owns a shop _____
2 a person who sells things in a shop _____
3 a person who sells things to shops _____
4 a reduction in price – for cash perhaps _____
5 a time when all the goods in a shop are cheaper _____
6 a place where all goods are cheaper (usually outside) _____
7 a group of shops together in one place _____
8 a big shop, with many different departments _____

B What's wrong?

We complain when something goes wrong with goods. The words we use to describe the problem change depending on the goods we are talking about.
What are we talking about when we say:

1 It's flat _____
2 It's blown _____
3 It's shrunk _____
4 It's faded _____
5 It's off _____
6 It's scratched _____
7 It's stained _____
8 It's run _____
9 It's out of tune _____
10 It's flickering _____

C In Authority

The person *in authority* in a shop is the <u>manager</u>.
Who is the person *in authority* in the cases below?

1 a football team _____
2 a tribe (of Red Indians, for example) _____
3 a company _____
4 a country _____
5 a hospital _____
6 an army _____
7 a school _____
8 a town in the Wild West! _____
9 a newspaper _____
10 a television studio _____

D Any delay will *weaken* your case.

Adjective + *en* = 'to make *adjective*'.
Which of the adjectives below can we make into verbs by adding *en*?

1 hard   2 soft   3 strong   4 wide
5 long   6 hot   7 cold   8 tight
9 loose   10 dark   11 bright   12 sure

What are the verbs meaning 'to make + *adjective*' for the rest?

84 Improving Your Vocabulary

E Change the verb.

The verbs in all these sentences are wrong. Can you change them round to make eight correct sentences?

1 The car nodded around the bend. _____
2 He pretended the coat from the peg. _____
3 The two gardens were unhooked by a wall. _____
4 The body covered on the ground. _____
5 The woman dented in agreement. _____
6 He disappeared to be reading a magazine. _____
7 The bus was separated in the accident. _____
8 The man lay the table with a cloth. _____

F ...in the middle of the gunroom floor...

a *gunroom* = a room where you keep guns
This noun is made up of two nouns: gun + room.
What do these similar words mean?

1 watchman _____
2 backbone _____
3 ballpoint _____
4 cloakroom _____
5 cottonwool _____
6 fireplace _____
7 lipstick _____
8 newsagent _____
9 nightfall _____
10 rainbow _____

If you have a **With Answers** edition, check pages 130–131 of the Key.

Unit 11 An English-Speaking World

A Talking about Space

Link the definitions on the left to the words on the right.

1	the world where we live	the moon
2	the thing that goes round it	the planets
3	the thing that shines on it	the solar system
4	the other members of the group	the Earth
5	the group of things together	outer space
6	the area outside this group	the sun
7	a plane which can travel there	the universe
8	everything that exists!	a spaceship

Improving Your Vocabulary 85

B Very, very, very...

In the text there are three words which mean very surprising:
   remarkable   extraordinary   astonishing

Do you know more words which mean...
1 very bad   4 very small
2 very nice   5 very clever
3 very big   6 very stupid

C Find the Verb.

Which of the verbs below goes in each space?

   list   conduct   store   transmit   comprehend

1 People   _____ languages.
2 Dictionaries _____ words.
3 Computers   _____ information.
4 Broadcasters _____ programmes.
5 Businessmen   _____ business.

D Incomprehensible

In the text it says that early English would be *incomprehensible* to modern ears, that is, we couldn't understand it.

Look how this is made up: not + comprehend + able
                             in   comprehens   ible

Note:
1 In English, the negative prefix takes many forms, as we saw before.
2 There are often spelling changes in putting these parts together.

Can you match the words to their meanings by drawing a line between them?

1 not able to see it   illegible
2 not able to hear it   inedible
3 not able to read it   illiterate
4 not able to eat it   inarticulate
5 not able to write   invisible
6 not able to express ideas   inaudible

7 What do we call a person who is not able to do something because of a physical problem?

E Nationality or Language or Both?

1 How many nationalities can you think of which are also languages
   For example: English, French, German...
2 Can you think of any cases where the word for the nationality is different from the word for the language?
   For example: Egyptian – Arabic; American – English

If you have a **With Answers** edition, check page 132 of the Key.

Unit 12 Coming to the UK

A Talking about Travel

There are many ways to travel. First, how do you start and finish?
Which of these verbs 1 – 7 can you use with the methods of transport? The first is done for you.

	ship	car	train	plane	bicycle
1 get on _____			✓	✓	✓
2 get in _____					
3 board _____					
4 mount _____					
5 alight from _____					
6 embark on _____					
7 catch/miss _____					

And when you are travelling, what are you doing?
  8 Write the action:

And who's the person in charge?
  9 Write the person:

And what's it called if you go for pleasure?
  10 Write the name:

B Head Words

It is very useful to know the head word – the set to which a word belongs.
Example: I *don't like cats, dogs...in fact, I don't like any pets.*
The word *pet* covers all animals kept by people for pleasure – not work.
Sometimes the head word helps you to explain another, more particular, word which you don't know.
Example: It's *a piece of <u>furniture</u> for the bedroom.*
Furniture covers *bed, chair, wardrobe,* etc., and helps the listener to know what you are talking about.
Find the head words for these groups:

1 cigarettes, cigars _____
2 beer, whisky, gin, wine _____
3 sheets, blankets, pillow cases _____
4 spanner, hammer, screwdriver, drill _____
5 football, cricket, rugby, baseball, tennis _____
6 chess, draughts, halma, mah-jong _____
7 lawyer, doctor, teacher, accountant _____
8 Islam, Christianity, Judaism, Buddhism _____
9 ship, plane, car, bus, train _____
10 geography, history, mathematics, biology _____

Try to add two more words to each of the lists above.

If you have a **With Answers** edition, check pages 132–133 in the Key.

SECTION 3 The Reading Texts

Unit 1 Mind that Child!

You are going to read a leaflet about road accidents. Choose the most suitable heading from the list **A – F** for the whole leaflet and for each section. There is one extra heading which you do not need to use.

A At which age are children most in danger?

B How are most road accidents caused?

C How many children are involved in road accidents?

D The facts about children and roads

E What can you do as a driver to make roads safer for children?

F Why are children more at risk?

1

2

∗ Road accidents are a major cause of death and injury to children. They account for a quarter of deaths of school children and for two thirds of all accidental deaths. In 1988, 462 children were killed in road accidents, and over 45,000 were injured.

3

∗ 1 in 15 children are injured in a road accident before their sixteenth birthday.

∗ Children in traffic are at far greater risk of an accident than adults.

∗ Children's observation and listening powers are less fully developed and their stature means they are less likely to see and be seen.

4

∗ The overall risk of an accident increases as a child gets older. As pedestrians the risk is greatest when children start secondary school.

∗ Most child pedestrians or cyclists who are killed or seriously injured are knocked down by cars on residential roads carrying only light traffic.

5

∗ Recognise all children can be:

    Immature
    Impulsive
    Unpredictable
    Lacking in skill and judgement
    Inexperienced
    Irresponsible
    Unable to judge speed and distances

∗ Drive slowly in residential areas, particularly where parked cars may obscure your view.

∗ Slow down when you see children, even if they are acting sensibly.

∗ Slow down when you see a children or school sign.

∗ Watch out for children wanting to cross at zebra or pelican crossings and when turning at junctions.

∗ Give child cyclists plenty of room.

Unit 2 The Train Journey

This case came before me quite by chance in the spring of last year. I was travelling out to Rome for a consultation. I might have saved time and fatigue if I had gone by air, but it was early in the year and I had decided against it on account of the high winds and rain. Instead, I booked a sleeper in the first class wagon-lit, and left Paris on the mid-day train.

The journey was a normal one as far as Dijon, and a little way beyond. But as the darkness fell and the line began to climb up into the Jura mountains the train went slower and slower, with frequent stops for no apparent reason. It was that difficult hour in a railway train, between tea and dinner, when one is tired of reading, reluctant to turn on the lights and face a long, dull evening, and conscious of no appetite at all to face another meal. It was raining a little; in the dusk the countryside seemed grey and depressing. The fact that the train was obviously becoming very late did not relieve the situation.

Presently we stopped again, and this time for a quarter of an hour. Then we began to move, but in the reverse direction. We ran backwards down the line at a slow speed, for perhaps a couple of miles, and drew into a little station in the woods that we had passed through some time previously. Here we stopped again, this time for good.

I was annoyed, and went out into the corridor to see if I could find out what was happening. There was a man there, a very tall, lean man, perhaps thirty-five or thirty-six years old. He was leaning out of the window. From his appearance, I guessed he was an Englishman, so I touched him on the shoulder and said: 'Do you know what's holding us up?'

Without turning he said: 'Half a minute.'

There was a good deal of shouting in French going on outside between the engine-driver, the guard, the head waiter of the restaurant car, and the various station officials. I speak French moderately, but I could make nothing of the broad, shouted vowels at the far end of the platform. My companion understood, however, for he drew back into the corridor and said:

'They're saying up there that there's a goods train off the lines between here and Frasne. We may have to stay here till the morning.'

Multiple Choice Comprehension Questions

1 The train was travelling...
   A from Paris to Dijon.
   B from Paris to Frasne.
   C from Rome to Paris.
   D from Paris to Rome.

2 The writer decided not to fly because...
   A it was spring.
   B there were high winds and rain.
   C it was early in the year.
   D he preferred travelling by train.

☐ 3 The train finally stopped...
   A before Dijon.
   B just after Dijon.
   C a couple of miles from a little station.
   D in the Jura mountains.

☐ 4 When the man said 'Half a minute'...
   A he was asking the writer to wait.
   B he was telling the writer the time.
   C he was explaining how long the delay would be.
   D he wanted the writer to help him.

☐ 5 The writer discovered the cause of the delay...
   A from the engine driver.
   B from his companion.
   C from the guard.
   D from the railway officials.

☐ 6 The delay to the writer's train was caused by...
   A a problem with the writer's train.
   B a problem with a train ahead.
   C an accident to a train ahead.
   D an accident between the writer's train and a goods train.

Unit 3 Green Lights

You are going to read some information about light bulbs. For Questions 1–10, choose from the type of bulbs **A – E**. Some of the types of bulbs may be chosen more than once. When more than one answer is required, these may be given in any order. There is an example at the beginning (**0**).

Which bulb or bulbs:

cost more than conventional bulbs	**0**	**A**
are good for general lighting	**1**	
are less expensive to run than conventional bulbs	**2**	
can be used with shades	**3**	**4**
cannot be dimmed by using a switch	**5**	
cost less than £10	**6**	
emit less carbon dioxide	**7**	
have ratings up to 25W	**8**	
are made by Philips and Osram	**9**	**10**

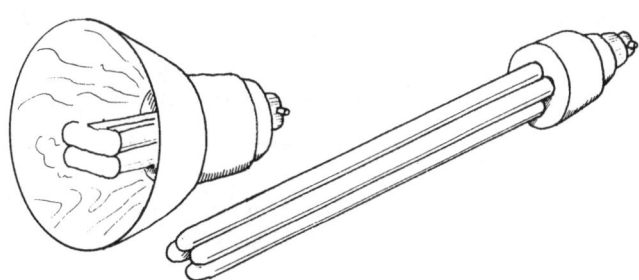

The Osram EL
pictured with reflector and globe

11 Where has this text come from?

A a brochure
B a government leaflet
C a consumer magazine
D an instruction leaflet

12 Why would someone read this text?

A to find out how the lights work
B to decide which type is most suitable for them
C to check the price of these lights
D to find out why the lights are more efficient

A

Energy-efficient light bulbs use up to 80% less electricity and save you around £30 during their lifetime. They cost more than conventional ones – up to £15 – but last up to eight times longer. Carbon dioxide emission is also reduced.

B

- Compact fluorescent bulbs work the same way as fluorescent tubes but are bulb-shaped, so they can be used with ordinary shades, but not with dimmer switches.

C

- Mazda Low Energy (14W) bulbs give white light for general lighting. They contain a separate, reusable adaptor and a plug-in bulb. This works out cheaper as only the bulb needs replacing. (From supermarkets and lighting specialists, £9.99 for bulb and adaptor; £5 for replacement bulb.)

D

- For softer light, look for Philips SL Decor and for the SL Compact range (both about £12). With a rating of 18W or 25W, these bulbs enclose the fluorescent tube in a glass cover. Also look for the Osram EL (7W, 11W, 15W, 20W), £14-17 – available with a reflector or a globe cover.

E

- For uplighters and wall lighters, look for Philips Electronic range (9W or 11W), about £15, or the Osram EL. The fluorescent tube gives a good strong light behind your shade.
- For a list of brands available by mail order, send a stamped sae to First Light, 28 Eastwood Road, Birmingham, B12 9NB.

OLD	NEW
FILAMENT	TUBE
Nearest equivalent	
100W	20W
75W	15W
60W	11W
40W	9W

Unit 4 Girls will be Girls

You are going to read a newspaper article about stereotyping. Five paragraphs have been removed from the article. Choose from the paragraphs **A – F** the one which fits each space **1 – 5**. There is one paragraph which you do not need to use.

A Washing clothes was only for women, said 85 per cent of boys and 86 per cent of girls. Repairing the car was for men, according to the majority of pupils.

B Boys and girls still see themselves as boys and girls, each with their own role to play. Most of them believe that boys repair cars while girls wash clothes, according to a new report published yesterday.

C Another said: 'The biggest problem area concerns our one computer. If this is on there are three boys who simply cannot keep their hands off it. I try to make sure those three are involved with something on the other side of the classroom, and do my best to encourage the girls – and the less confident boys – to use it.'

D The report recommends that teachers should be made aware of the danger of sexual stereotyping; that girls be helped to involve themselves in science and technology; and that more men should be employed in infants' schools.

E Even where children have seen jobs being done by both sexes, such as teaching young children and doctors, there is still a tendency to believe in stereotypes, the former viewed as a preserve for women and the latter mainly for men.

F Sexual stereotyping is still common in working life. It is still unusual to find women as bank managers, chief executives of large companies or surgeons. It cannot be because fewer women enter these professions. If anything, there are more women than men working in banking and medicine.

Girls will be girls and boys will be boys...

1

Children aged five and six have inherited the attitudes of their grandparents, which are preventing more women from becoming scientists and engineers, says the report.

2

Wearing trousers, shopping, and looking after somebody who is ill are the three roles most popularly considered to be right for both men and women, but children believe that only men should be scientists, says the report, commissioned by the National Association of Schoolmasters, the Union of Women Teachers and the Engineering Council.

The survey of 259 boys, 247 girls and 218 teachers, shows that divisions between the sexes exist despite modern attitudes and the national curriculum. Some people even consider the substitution of chairperson for chairman as sexist, says the report from Manchester University. Mending the car, fire-fighting, climbing mountains, woodwork and being a scientist are all seen as men-only activities by most girls and boys. Hairdressing, mending clothes, cooking, wearing jewellery and doing the laundry are almost exclusively for women.

3

Only one teacher told the researchers: 'The boys tend to exclude girls from some playground games and think they should be allowed to reserve some equipment for their own use, such as a train or garage set. Some boys automatically assumed that the girls would take on the role of nurses in hospital play and cast themselves in the role of doctors.'

4

Most teachers said they tried to counteract stereotyping, with 83.8 per cent saying they did, 12.1 per cent saying they did not and 3.5 per cent saying there was no need.

About two-thirds of teachers believed the national curriculum would help to reduce the problem, a quarter said that it would not and nearly 12 per cent said they did not know.

5

Unit 5 Home Improvement Loans

1 Where has this text come from?

A an advertisement
B an article in a financial journal
C an information leaflet
D a magazine article

2 Why would someone read this text?

A if they wanted to borrow money
B if they wanted to buy a house
C if they wanted a fitted kitchen
D if they wanted free Marks and Spencer vouchers

HOME IMPROVEMENT LOANS

TURN YOUR HOUSE INTO A MORE COMFORTABLE HOME.

Haven't you waited long enough for that fitted kitchen?

Isn't it high time you did that loft conversion?

And how long have you been promising to give the bedroom a facelift?

Whatever home improvement you have in mind, you can afford it now with a loan from First National Bank. You can borrow any sum from £7,500.

Your loan will be secured by a mortgage on your property which means a lower rate of interest and a longer time to repay.

If you take out £7,500 over 180 months your monthly repayment at APR 21.5% variable will be £129.96 – and the total amount payable £23,392.80.

Take out £15,000 or more and you'll be able to benefit from an even lower rate of interest (currently APR 19.7% variable).

How can we afford to do it? We may be one of the country's leading consumer banks with group assets in excess of £1.7 billion but we don't ask you to pay for expensive overheads like High Street branches because all our transactions are arranged speedily by post. We can also afford to give you valuable peace of mind.

For example, if you're under 60 you get Free Life Assurance on the total amount you owe up to £15,000.

There is even a special plan which enables you to insure your repayments – in case of illness, an accident or redundancy – for just a few pounds a month.

If you need any further incentive, on completion of your loan, we'll give you £150 worth of Marks & Spencer vouchers to help with those finishing touches. However, this offer closes 31st July 1991.

Call us **FREE ON 0800 850 850** any week day, 9.00am to 9.00pm and weekends 10am to 5pm, for an immediate quote and decision. Or you can fill in the straightforward application form and everything will be quickly arranged by post.

The information is totally confidential and you won't pay a penny in arrangement fees.

APR	MONTHLY REPAYMENTS			APR
	LOAN AMOUNT	60 MONTHS	120 MONTHS	180 MONTHS	
19.7 VARIABLE	£15,000	£381.89	£271.44	£242.86	19.7 VARIABLE
	£10,000	£263.17	£191.14	£173.27	
21.5 VARIABLE	£7,500	£197.38	£143.36	£129.96	21.5 VARIABLE

FREE. £150 WORTH OF MARKS & SPENCER VOUCHERS.

CALL FREE ON 0800 850 850

FIRST NATIONAL BANK — THE LENDING BANK

Multiple Choice Comprehension Questions

3 You can borrow money from First National Bank…

A to buy a fitted kitchen.
B to convert your loft.
C for anything you want.
D for any home improvement.

☐ 4 You can only borrow money from First National Bank...
   A if you have a mortgage.
   B if you own a house.
   C if you are a tenant.
   D if you are married.

☐ 5 What is the minimum you can borrow?
   A £10,000
   B £15,000
   C £7,500
   D There is no minimum.

☐ 6 What is the maximum you can borrow?
   A £1.7 billion
   B £7,500
   C £15,000
   D more than £15,000

☐ 7 You can insure your repayments in case of illness, accident or redundancy...
   A if you are under 60.
   B if you are ill.
   C if you pay a few pounds extra.
   D if you borrow £15,000

☐ 8 If you want to borrow money...
   A you can phone or send the application form.
   B you must send the application form.
   C you must phone.
   D you must make an appointment.

Unit 6 The Kennedy Conspiracy

You are going to read part of a book about an assassination. Seven sentences have been removed from the text. Choose from the sentences **A – H** which fits each space **1 – 7**. There is one extra sentence which you do not need to use.

A 'We've almost got it made.'
B 'My God, I'm hit!'
C 'Mr Kennedy, you can't say Dallas doesn't love you.'
D 'The President ought to be awarded the Purple Heart just for coming to Dallas.'
E 'Don't worry about it. It's going to be a great trip.'
F 'I'm really looking forward to my visit.'
G 'I wish I weren't going to Dallas.'
H 'Dallas is a very dangerous place. I wouldn't go there.'

In his office at the White House, the President looked gloomily across the desk at his press secretary. **1**, he said. The secretary replied, **2**.

It was November 20, 1963. The President had received warnings about Dallas from all sides. Senator William Fulbright had told him, **3**. That morning Senator Hubert Humphrey had advised him not to go.

The President knew he had to go. Dallas, a thousand miles away, had voted overwhelmingly for Richard Nixon in the last presidential election. This time round, the state of Texas as a whole was sure to be tough territory for the Democrats, and Kennedy was determined to take the initiative.

On November 21 the President flew south from Washington to San Antonio, his first stop of the Texas tour. All went well there, and Kennedy made a speech about the space age. He went on to Houston and talked about the space program again ...

November 22 began with a speech in the rain and a political breakfast. Just before noon, the President arrived in Dallas. There were welcoming crowds at the airport and then he was travelling to the city centre in an open limousine. As Kennedy passed, one spectator said to her husband, **4**.

At 12.29 pm the motorcade was amidst cheering crowds, moving slowly through the metal and glass canyons of central Dallas.

For a while, there had been no talking in the President's car. Then, with the passing crowd a kaleidoscope of welcome, the wife of the Governor of Texas turned to smile at the President. **5**.

Ponderously, at eleven miles an hour, the procession moved on to Elm Street and into an open space. This was Dealey Plaza, a wide expanse of grass stretching away to the left of the cars. To the right of the President towered the Texas School Book Depository, a warehouse, the last high building in this part of the city. In the lead car an officer looked ahead at a railway tunnel and said to a colleague, **6**. It was now twelve seconds past 12.30 pm.

Then several shots rang out in rapid succession. According to a Secret Serviceman in the car, the President said, **7**.

Unit 7 The Disease Detectives

'We live in muck and filth,' they wrote to the London Times on July 3, 1849, in a letter signed by 54 of that city's poor.* 'We haven't got any toilets, no dustbins, no drains, no water supplies, and there is no sewer in the whole place... We all suffer, and many of us are ill, and if the cholera comes Lord help us.' Five years later, in 1854, cholera came with a vengeance.

A man walking in good health, it was said, could be dead by sundown. Within 250 yards of the intersection of Cambridge and Broad Streets, more than 500 people died in little more than a week. Carts groaned under the weight of corpses carried away for mass burial. Those who could, fled. Others locked themselves away in fear.

No one knew how or why contagions spread. Some blamed foul vapours. Others saw the work of divine retribution. Decades would pass before medical scientists accepted the idea that microbes too small to see were the cause of infection.

But a 41-year-old physician named John Snow believed he had found the source of the Broad Street contagion. On a map of London, Snow marked where victims died. Nearly all the deaths, he saw, had taken place near the Broad Street pump – one of many public water pumps in London.

But before he could be sure, Snow had to understand why ten deaths had occurred nearer another street pump. Amid the growing panic, Snow visited the families of the deceased. Five of the distant victims, he learned, regularly sent for water from the pump at Broad Street, preferring its taste. Three others were children who attended a school near Broad Street's pump.

That was all he needed. On September 7, Snow appeared before the vestry of St. James's Parish, meeting in solemn consultation on the causes of the epidemic. His request astonished them. He asked that the Broad Street pump handle be removed. It was. Within days the outbreak of cholera ended.

Although Snow did not discover cholera's cause – a bacterium called Vibrio cholera – his methodical work helped establish modern epidemiology, 'the art and science' as one of his present day counterparts would put it, 'of chasing epidemics'.

*The original text is as follows:

'We live in muck and filthe,' they wrote to the London *Times* on July 3, 1849, in a letter signed by 54 of that city's poor. 'We aint got no priviz, no dust bins, no drains, no water-splies, and so suer in the hole place... We all of us suffur, and numbers are ill, and if the Colera comes Lord help us.'

Multiple Choice Comprehension Questions

1   The cholera epidemic in London in 1854 was caused by...
   A   the muck and filth.
   B   the foul vapours.
   C   the water from the Broad Street pump.
   D   the handle of the Broad Street pump.

2   Many deaths occurred...
   A   in Cambridge.
   B   near the Broad Street pump.
   C   before sundown.
   D   in carts.

3   John Snow found the cause of the outbreak...
   A   by taking the handle off the Broad Street pump.
   B   by visiting families of the deceased.
   C   by appearing before the vestry of St. James's parish.
   D   by marking where the victims died on a map.

4   In the 1850s people thought cholera was caused by...
   A   dirty conditions.
   B   microbes too small to see.
   C   a bacterium called *Vibrio cholera*.
   D   the Broad Street pump.

5   John Snow's work is important today because...
   A   he discovered the cause of cholera.
   B   he discovered the cause of epidemics in general.
   C   he established the art and science of chasing epidemics.
   D   he used methods which are the basis of modern epidemiology.

Unit 8 Fire!

You are going to read a leaflet about fire. Choose the most suitable heading from the list **A – G** for each space **1 – 6**. There is one extra heading which you do not need to use.

A Deaths in fires
B Don't panic...fight back!
C Fires in the home
D Get down...and stay down
E How to survive a hotel fire
F If you are forced to stay in your room
G Smoke or fire?

1

2

Contrary to what you may have seen on television or in the movies, fire is not likely to burn you to death. It's the by-products of fire that will kill you. Super heated fire gases (smoke) and panic will almost always be the cause of death long before the fire arrives, if it ever does. This is very important. You must know how to avoid smoke and panic to survive a hotel fire. With this in mind, here are a few tips.

3

Where there is smoke there is not necessarily fire. A smouldering mattress, for instance, will produce great amounts of smoke. Air conditioning and air exchange systems will sometimes pick up smoke from one room and carry it to other rooms or floors. You should keep that in mind because 70 per cent of hotel fires are caused by smoking and matches.

In any case, your prime objective should be to leave the hotel at the first signs of smoke.

4

Smoke, being warmer, will start accumulating at the ceiling and work its way down. The first thing you will notice is there are no 'exit' signs.

Another thing about smoke you should be aware of is how irritating it is on the eyes. The problem is your eyes will take only so much irritation, then they close. Try all you want, you won't be able to open them if there is still smoke in the area.

Lastly, the fresh air you want to breathe is at or near the floor. Get on your hands and knees (or stomach) and STAY THERE as you make your way out. Those who don't probably won't get that far.

5

Should you wake up to smoke in your room and the door is too hot to open or the hallway is completely charged with smoke, don't panic. Many people have defended themselves quite nicely in their rooms and so can you. One of the first things you'll want to do is open the window to vent the smoke. If there is fresh air outside, leave the window open, but keep an eye on it. At this point, most people would stay at the window, waving frantically, while their room continues to fill with smoke or the fire burns through. You must be aggressive and fight back.

6

Here are some things you can do in any order you choose: If the room phone works, let someone know you're in there. Flip on the bathroom vent. Fill the tub with water. Wet some sheets or towels and stuff the cracks of your door to keep out smoke. With your ice bucket, bail water from the bathtub on the door to keep it cool. Feel the walls; if they're hot, bail water on them too. You can put your mattress up against the door and block it in place with the chest. Keep it wet: keep everything wet. A wet towel tied around your nose and mouth is an effective halter if you fold it in a triangle and put the corner in your mouth. The point is, there shouldn't be any reason to panic; keep fighting until reinforcements arrive. It won't be long.

Unit 9 Death in the Family

You are going to read an extract from a novel. Seven sentences have been removed from the extract. Choose from the sentences **A – H** the one which fits each gap **1 – 6**. There is one extra sentence which you do not need to use. There is an example at the beginning (**0**).

> A 'He just went to sleep.'
>
> B 'You'll get another dog, I suppose?'
>
> C Alec Chipstead looked around for something to put over it.
>
> D Alec put it into his pocket.
>
> E Alec said, no, thanks, really, he'd see to all that.
>
> F Alec went back into the house.
>
> G Alec went outside to see the vet off.
>
> H How long had that been there?

The body lay on a small square of carpet in the middle of the gun-room floor. **0 C** He unhooked a raincoat from one of the pegs and, covering the body, reflected too late that he would never wear that again.
1
'I'm glad that's all over.'
'Extraordinary how painful these things can be,' said the vet. **2**
'I expect so. That's really up to Meg.'
The vet nodded. He got into his car, put his head out of the window and asked Alec if he was sure he didn't want the body taken away. **3** He watched the car move off, up the long, sloping lane that in those parts was called a drift, under the overhanging branches of the trees, and disappear round a bend where the pine wood began.
On the edge of the grass, where a strip of flower border separated it from the paved drive, lay a rubber ball dented with toothmarks. **4** Months probably. It was a long time since Fred had been up to playing with a ball.
5 He walked round the house, up the stone steps onto the terrace and in by the French windows.
Meg was sitting in the drawing room, pretending to read *Country Life*.
'He didn't know a thing,' Alec said. **6**
'What fools we are.'
'I held him on my lap and he went to sleep and the vet gave him the injection and he – died.'

Unit 10 How to Complain

You are going to read a leaflet about complaints. Choose the most suitable heading from the list **A – H** for each space **1 – 7**. There is one extra heading which you do not need to use.

A Be polite but firm
B Complain as soon as possible
C How to complain about goods
D How to complain about services
E Know what you want
F Make your complaint to the right person
G Manufacturer or retailer?
H Take a receipt

1

A typical example: you buy a pair of shoes in a sale. A week later a strap comes right away making the shoes unwearable. What should you do?

2

Although there is no obligation on you to return the goods, it is best to take them back as soon as you discover the defect. If it is impractical for you to return to the shop at once, perhaps because you live a long way off, or because the goods are bulky, write to say that you are dissatisfied with the product and ask for collection arrangements to be made. Any unexplained or unreasonable delay will weaken your case.

3

Many people believe that the initial complaint about faulty goods should be made to the manufacturer. This is not the case. Your contract is with the retailer, the party who sold you the goods, and so it is to him that your complaint should be made.

HOW TO COMPLAIN

4

It is always a good idea to ask for the manager in a shop or the departmental manager in a large store. In asking for a person in authority you also show that you mean business right from the start. Don't be fobbed off with the common response that the manager is 'in a meeting' or 'away'. Insist that someone must have been left in charge and that you'll see that person. Failing that, register your complaint with the assistant and make an appointment to call back and see the manager at a mutually convenient time.

5

When making your complaint it is important that you adopt the right tone. The last thing you want to do is antagonise the person you are dealing with. You should try to be polite but firm and give a generally businesslike impression. Maintain this approach and avoid having a row.

6

It is remarkable how many people return faulty products to the seller not having the faintest idea what they want to happen. Do you want a full refund, a repair, a credit note or an exchange? You may not get what you want but you should decide beforehand.

7

Wherever possible try to take your receipt back with the goods. A receipt can prove that the goods were bought from a particular shop or store. A shop will want to make sure that the goods were bought there before considering your complaint. However, you are not legally obliged to show a receipt. You may have some other proof of purchase: for example, you may have a cheque stub or credit card voucher, or a particular trader's name may be stitched or stamped on to the product or an assistant may remember you, or you may have had someone with you when you bought the goods.

Unit 11 An English-Speaking World

On 5 September 1977, the American spacecraft Voyager One blasted off on its historic mission to Jupiter and beyond. On board, the scientists, who knew that Voyager would one day spin through distant star systems, had installed a recorded greeting from the people of the planet Earth. Preceding a brief message in fifty-five different languages for the people of outer space, the gold-plated disc plays a statement, from the Secretary-General of the United Nations, an Austrian named Kurt Waldheim, speaking on behalf of 147 member states – in English.

The rise in English is a remarkable story. When Julius Caesar landed in Britain nearly two thousand years ago, English did not exist. Five hundred years later, *Englisc*, incomprehensible to modern ears, was probably spoken by about as few people as currently speak Cherokee – and with about as little influence. Nearly a thousand years later, at the end of the sixteenth century, when William Shakespeare was in his prime, English was the native speech of between five and six million Englishmen and it was, in the words of a contemporary, 'of small reach, it stretches no further than this island of ours, no, not there over all'.

Four hundred years later, the contrast is extraordinary. Between 1600 and the present, in armies, navies, companies and expeditions, the speakers of English – including Scots, Irish, Welsh, American and many more – travelled into every corner of the globe, carrying their language and culture with them. Today, English is used by at least 750 million people, and barely half of those speak it as a mother tongue. Some estimates have put that figure closer to one billion. Whatever the total, English at the end of the twentieth century is more widely scattered, more widely spoken and written, than any other language has ever been. It has become the language of the planet, the first truly global language.

The statistics are astonishing. Of all the world's languages (which now number some 2700), it is arguably the richest in vocabulary. The *Oxford English Dictionary* lists about 500,000 words; and a further half million technical and scientific terms remain uncatalogued. According to traditional estimates, neighbouring German has a vocabulary of about 185,000 words and French fewer than 100,000. About 350 million people use the English vocabulary as a mother tongue: about one-tenth of the world's population.

Three-quarters of the world's mail, and its telexes and cables, are in English. So are more than half the world's technical and scientific periodicals: it is the language of technology from Silicon Valley to Shanghai. English is the medium for 80 per cent of the information stored in the world's computers. Nearly half of all business deals in Europe are conducted in English. Five of the largest broadcasting companies in the world transmit in English to audiences that regularly exceed one hundred million.

Multiple Choice Comprehension Questions

1. Voyager One carried...
    - A scientists and a gold-plated disc.
    - B a recorded greeting from Kurt Waldheim.
    - C a message on behalf of the United Nations.
    - D a speech in 55 different languages.

2. The English language has existed for...
    - A over two thousand years.
    - B since Shakespeare was in his prime.
    - C four hundred years.
    - D over fifteen hundred years.

3. English spread around the world in the last 400 years because...
    - A there were many armies, navies, companies and expeditions.
    - B people travelled to every corner of the globe.
    - C the Scots, Irish, Welsh and Americans spoke English.
    - D English speakers from many countries travelled widely.

4. English is a global language because...
    - A there are so many native speakers.
    - B so many people use it as a second language
    - C it has probably got the largest vocabulary of any language.
    - D it has many native and non-native speakers.

5. English is used for...
    - A seventy-five per cent of the world's mail.
    - B nearly fifty per cent of the world's technical and scientific magazines.
    - C nearly half of the world's business deals.
    - D nearly three quarters of the information stored in computers.

Unit 12 Coming to the UK

You are going to read some information for travellers to the UK. For Questions **1 – 10**, choose from the sections **A – E** the one you need to read in each case. Some of the sections may be chosen more than once. When more than one answer is required, these may be given in any order. There is an example at the beginning (**0**).

Which section or sections should you read if…

you want to bring in cigarettes?	**0**	**A**
you are bringing in goods to resell in the UK?	**1**	
you are coming to study in the UK?	**2**	**3**
you are moving permanently to the UK from an EC country?	**4**	
you are a tourist bringing in personal clothing?	**5**	
you are visiting the UK for more than 6 months?	**6**	
you have just got married to a person resident in England?	**7**	
you want to bring in your own car?	**8**	**9**
you want to bring in your dog?	**10**	

INFORMATION ALL TRAVELLERS NEED TO KNOW

1. General Information
(See Section 2 for the meaning of certain words)

What is this notice about?
It tells you about bringing your belongings through UK Customs and which of these may be imported free of duty and tax.

A	**Duty-free allowances**

In addition to the reliefs in Section 4 to 7, you can have the allowances for alcoholic drinks, tobacco products, perfume and toilet water and other goods (popularly known as 'duty frees'). These are listed in our Notice 1 and are shown on the display posters in the baggage halls.

If you are moving your home to the UK from within the EC, you may qualify for an extra (though limited) amount of alcoholic drink and tobacco products as explained in paragraph 22.

B	**Pets**

Your pet can count as part of your belongings, but you must see paragraph 4 about the restrictions on importing live animals, fish and birds. You must fill in a Form C3 for each pet.

11 Where has this text come from?

A a government leaflet
B a travel brochure
C a tourist guide
D a consumer magazine

12 Who would read this text?

A a lawyer
B a tourist in the USA
C a person who is planning to come to the UK
D the manager of an import–export company

C	Prohibited and restricted goods

Don't be tempted to import illegally any prohibited or restricted goods. These are listed in our Notice 2.

Other Customs notices

You may need to look at other Customs notices if you are:
- bringing in a private motor vehicle – see Notice 3A;
- bringing in a pleasure craft – see Notice 8 or 8A;
- moving to the UK on marriage – see Notice 4;
- bringing in inherited goods – see Notice 368;
- bringing in antiques – see Notice 362.

2. Visiting the UK

For everyone who usually lives outside the UK and does not intend to move their normal home to the UK. Students whose normal home is outside the UK count as visitors.

D	Rules of the relief

As a visitor your belongings can be free of duty and tax and need not be declared to the Customs so long as:

- all belongings are brought in with you and are for your use alone;
and
- they are kept in the UK for no more than 6 months in a 12-month period;
and
- you do NOT sell, lend, hire out or otherwise dispose of them in the UK;
and
- they are exported either:
  – when you leave the UK; or
  – before they have been in the UK for more than 6 months, WHICHEVER HAPPENS FIRST.

For private motor vehicles, see Notice 3A.

E	Students

Students who usually live outside the UK can temporarily import belongings under the relief in paragraph D.

In addition, if you are on a full-time course of study at a school, college or university, you can permanently import, free of duty and tax, for your own personal use, your:

- clothing and household linen;
and
- articles for use in your studies;
and
- household effects for furnishing your rooms.

These items must be declared as explained in paragraph 10.